GW01072025

The Inspector Calls:
Confessions of a police speaker!

Neil Sadler

First Published 2021
by
Independent Publishing Network / Neil Sadler

Printed and bound in the UK by
Lemonade Print Group Ltd
www.lemonadeprint.com

Neil trained as a school teacher and worked on the Isle of Man before returning to England for a very brief spell as a civil servant based in Bristol. In 1978 he decided that an office based job was not for him and he joined Sussex Police.

Much of his 30 years service was as an operational officer in various ranks across Sussex. He also worked briefly in Hong Kong, Trinidad and Abu Dhabi….and even survived Bognor Regis, Haywards Heath and Crawley!

Following retirement in 2008, he now offers his talks to groups and organisations throughout Sussex, Surrey, Kent, Hampshire and south London.

Neil lives in West Sussex with his long-suffering wife, Julie, to whom he will be forever grateful.

Recent bookings for live talks have included:

- Local History Societies, Civic and preservation societies
- National Trust Associations; Active Retirement Assoc groups in Kent
- Royal British Legion; Oddfellows; Masonic groups
- Probus Clubs; male, female and mixed lunches
- u3a groups; NAWC; National Health retirement groups
- Women's Institutes in East and West Sussex, Surrey, Kent and Hampshire
  (accredited speaker)

Neil can be contacted via: **neilsadler1953@gmail.com**

My thanks to my good friend Andy Harrison for the artwork on the cover. This was a gift on my 50th birthday........quite some years ago !

To the memory of all my police colleagues, alive and passed, I reproduce the following anonymous poem.

The Police

I have been where you fear to be. I have seen what you fear to see

I have done what you fear to do.   All these things I have done for you

I am the man you lean upon.   The man you cast your scorn upon

The man you bring your troubles to.   All these men I've been to you

The man you ask to stand apart.   The man you feel should have no heart.

The man you call the man in blue.   But I'm just a man, just like you.

And through the years I've come to see. That I'm not what you ask of me

So take this badge and truncheon too.   Will you take it? Any one of you?

And when you watch a person die.   And hear a battered child cry

Then do you think that you can be. All the things you ask of me.

Contents

The inspector calls: confessions of a police speaker

Introduction

The distinguished gentleman stood to deliver his vote of thanks at the end of my talk. "I am, no doubt, the only person in this room who has seen Neil totally naked!" he said, to looks of surprise from the mixed audience. He qualified his comments very quickly, explaining that he had actually been my family doctor for over twenty years!

Retiring from Sussex Police in 2008 after thirty years, I was really looking forward to working on a casual basis at police recruit assessment centres. Sadly, the 2010 general election put paid to that idea, as all recruitment ground to a sudden halt. Austerity had set in.

I soon realised I needed something to occupy my days (and give my long- suffering wife, Julie, a break!). I had spent some time in national police training, so the thought gradually emerged of developing a variety of talks, as most people seem to enjoy "cops and robber" stories.

Little did I know that in order to be able to talk at Women's Institute meetings I needed to attend *and pass* an audition, not dissimilar from being on X Factor.

The day arrived and I attended my first audition (or speaker selection day) in Polegate village hall near Eastbourne. I had wrongly assumed there would be just a handful of ladies sitting around a trestle table, we would have a brief chat, a cup of tea and then I would go home. I was amazed to find 130 ladies sitting in rows awaiting my "sample performance", all with marking sheets to score my efforts!

I had been allocated the slot just before lunch, hence there were very few questions at the end: lunchtime sandwiches and flasks of soup awaited. Fortunately, I was accepted.

My advice after four separate speaker audition days for four different counties is to pick a simple section which is quick and easy to deliver. At one audition I made the big mistake of choosing "The rise of Robo-cop"; changes in police uniform and equipment.

I spent the first five minutes of my very brief twenty minute slot trying to explain that "Robo-cop" had been an American film about a good guy vigilante.

Wind the clock forward eight years and I have been lucky enough to receive many bookings from a wide variety of different organisations, from as far afield as Andover in Hampshire across to Dartford in Kent, plus many in south London.

I have developed a variety of talks (three are police related). The first one is called "A policeman's lot…can be quite an interesting one". Another is entitled "Gongoozling for beginners" and is a light hearted "cruise" through some of the most beautiful countryside in the UK, touching on the practicalities of living aboard a canal narrowboat, especially when things don't go exactly to plan!

What I really enjoy is meeting nice people, in nice places who actually want to see me; unlike many times during my 30 years police service. Venues have been as diverse as a south London Synagogue, a Sussex church and a Unitarian Meeting House, not to mention numerous village halls and the odd pub.

At one such hall I was to be followed two days later by a lady whose talk was entitled *"My life as a Playboy Bunny-girl!"*: variety is certainly the spice of life in *that* village.

Feedback often provides me with a smile. Examples have included: "Very well received: one of our members who regularly falls asleep during talks did not do so on this occasion!" and "...short, sharp stories, kept their attention (the first time they have kept so quiet!")

People never cease to surprise me when they come up and speak to me at the end of a talk. From the lady who told me her great grandfather was a mounted policeman at the Great Exhibition of 1851 to the elderly gentleman in Brighton who came and gave me his somewhat forthright views on Margaret Thatcher and her attitude to the miners' strike in 1984. I will also never forget the elderly lady at a regional WI meeting who whispered to me "Before you leave dear, will you handcuff me. I have always wondered what it felt like!"

I suggested she may have been reading too many books like *50 Shades of Grey* and promptly excused myself. As I said, I am still meeting some interesting people.

Chapter 1

Why write it down now?

I never intended to put into print the contents of my various talks. It seemed for a long time to be counter-productive to do so, as people could just get hold of the book, read it and have no need to book me to deliver a talk. The old adage "Killing the goose that lays the golden egg" sprang to mind.

However, that all changed in mid-March 2020, following the outbreak of what became known as Coronavirus / Covid -19 in Wuhan province, China which spread rapidly across the globe.

Suddenly, something which began as a fairly low priority TV news story about an outbreak in a far- off country, became the dominating and almost sole item of news in the UK.

Television channels, print and social media went into overdrive about the terrible toll this new virus was taking. Firstly in China, south Korea, Iran and then, much closer to home in Italy. Then Spain followed suit and the death rate began climbing. In the first weeks of March 2020, reported cases were restricted to those who had either visited south east Asia or northern states of Italy. But, of course, the world is so interconnected it was inevitable that virtually every nation would experience its own outbreak, to a greater or lesser extent.

The UK was no different and, night after night, the Prime Minister, Boris Johnson, told the nation the latest measures the government was taking to limit the outbreak, not least for the most vulnerable in society. Not surprisingly, these included the elderly and those with what became known as "underlying or pre-existing health issues"

I had been very fortunate that since my first successful speakers' selection days in 2012, bookings for talks had risen steadily, year on year. I put this down to my entries in the Women's Institute speakers' year books and spreading by word of mouth. This happened when wives would tell their husbands about me and a gentlemens' group, such as PROBUS would contact me at some later date.

Bearing in mind the average age profile of most of my client groups, it was no great surprise when the phone started ringing in early March 2020 with the same thing in common.

"Due to the government advice about the corona virus outbreak, I am sorry but we have had to cancel our meeting". It became such a frequent event that I even typed up a little pre-formatted memo to email back to apologetic bookings secretaries:

> *"Hello and many thanks for updating me. I must admit I am not surprised based on the current situation we find ourselves in*
>
> *Please get back in touch "post- hibernation" and I look forward to joining you in happier, less stressful times. In the meantime, keep healthy and smiling...where possible.*
>
> *Best wishes   Neil Sadler*

So essentially, this book is a collection of some of my experiences over thirty years as a police officer, followed by the next stage of my life as a public speaker talking about those experiences. Or, as my wife so kindly puts it, parodying the Mastermind candidates' personal introductions;

"Neil Sadler...specialist subject: Himself ! "

I had always thought I would write down the contents of my talks one day, but not until I had finished delivering them personally. This I reckoned would be after I had reached say talk number 1500 or when I got bored with doing them. However, my enforced "hibernation" gave me the opportunity to knuckle down and start it now.

In late May 2020 the oldest man in the world passed away. His name was Bob Weighton and he was 112 years of age. He had been born in Hull in 1908 and was survived by two children, ten grandchildren and an amazing twenty five great grand children. I mention Bob for a couple of reasons. In an interview with the BBC he told the reporter he considered laughter to be extremely important.

He said "I think most of the trouble in the world is caused by people taking themselves too seriously". He also said the secret to his longevity was "to avoid dying". He sounded quite a card.

I was reminded of Bob when I was typing many of the anecdotes you will read shortly. Black or gallows humour has long been recognised as having therapeutic value, particularly when used by individuals dealing with traumatic incidents.

With this in mind, it is no surprise this type of humour is commonly used by people working in the emergency services. It is a bona fide coping mechanism which can contribute to the resilience and wellbeing of emergency services personnel but one which, to the uninitiated, may appear callous and uncaring. Essentially, it is really just a mechanism people develop to "get through the shift and come back tomorrow".

A classic example of this occurred when I was being tutored in my first few weeks of service. My crew mate that morning, Basil, was a hard- bitten Glaswegian with many years police service who had transferred to Sussex for a better family life.

We were called to the scene of a road crash where a refuse collector had stepped out from behind his vehicle and been struck by a passing car. Sadly, he was killed instantly. It was now our task to visit the victim's home and inform his wife of the tragedy.

"OK son, let's have a practice as this will be your first death message" said Basil sternly. "What is the best way to approach this, Basil?" I asked, hoping for some supportive words from a veteran. "Well, you ask the woman if she is the widow Brown. When she replies No, you just say, well you are now". Basil roared with laughter when he saw my horrified expression. Luckily, when the time came Basil was the height of compassion, as I had hoped he would be.

Where appropriate, I have added the strange, funny or poignant things people have said to me at various police talks. These appear in text boxes as **Talks experience.**

Earlier, I mentioned my wife, Julie and her joking reference to me liking to talk about myself.

It is generally agreed that rates of divorce are particularly high in certain professions. This can be attributed to poor work / life balance, the amount of stress caused in the workplace and accumulated trauma experienced on a regular basis. In fact, when I attended my last Police Federation conference in 2008 I just happened to pick up a "freebie" off one of the stands.

I had been attracted to the nice blue colour of the complimentary glass mug, but was also intrigued by the advertising logo on it. WWW.POLICEDIVORCE.CO.UK.

I decided to check out the website as research for this book. It didn't compute. But the company who had produced this eye-catching item in 2008 still existed. They are called Gorvins and are a family law firm. Their website had a complete section on "Divorce and relationship breakdown for police".

They tell prospective clients, "At Gorvins our experienced police family law team have worked with police federation members and police officers for many years helping them during this very sensitive time on issues such as child arrangements and asset division". Having said all this, over my thirty years service I came across more colleagues who had stayed married than had divorced. But work place pressures *can* put an immense strain on a police officer's personality and relationships.

What I am trying to say is that I am extremely grateful for the stable home life Julie, my wife, was able to provide for me and our three children. It could not have been easy keeping small children quiet whilst "Daddy slept" after seven straight night shifts, or dealing with the mood swings caused by tiredness, unwanted telephone calls for advice at 3am or flashbacks to the murdered teenager who had been kicked to death on an innocent night out in Crawley. Thank you.

Chapter 2

How it all began

For some reason which I still can't recall, I trained as a school teacher between 1972-76. Perhaps the ratio of 100 male students to 400 female students had some bearing on my choice of Newton Park College of Education, near the historic city of Bath. My first and, as it turned out, only job in the teaching profession, was at a large primary school just outside Douglas, the capital of the Isle of Man.

Whilst this seemed quite attractive at the interview held during the long hot summer of 1976, I soon realised that out of season the Isle of Man, can be a somewhat limiting and isolating place, especially when you have no family or friends living on the island. This was made all the worse if the scheduled flights were unable to take off from Ronaldsway airport due to low lying mist, technical issues, etc.

Little wonder that some of us *"Comeovers"* (as Manx people named folks who had crossed the Irish sea to live and work on *their* island), gave the island a similarly affectionate nick name. The name *"Alca-Man"* compared the mist shrouded island in the Irish sea with the US penitentiary of Alcatraz in San Francisco harbour.

It didn't take long for me to realise I had made a big mistake with teaching as my chosen profession. By nature, I am not a particularly patient person. Neither did I enjoy the constant pressure of prepare-teach-mark-prepare etc.

Although he later went on to deny it, a fellow teacher of some seniority at the school sidled up to me on my very first day. I shall never forget his advice. In whispered tones so the head master could not hear him: "Whatever you do, if you don't like teaching, get out quickly... I wish I had done". After two years (or more accurately just five terms) I was sitting at my desk one Monday morning, having collected all the milk money and dinner money from my class of eight year olds. I looked out at a sea of thirty-eight little Manx faces and the thought struck me "God, I can't stand kids!"

Now that probably isn't the best thought to have with the next forty years in the classroom to look forward to. I decided to resign at that very moment and left with no regrets at Easter 1978.

Coming back to the mainland, I blundered into a job which had absolutely nothing to do with children. Sadly, it had everything to do with bureaucracy, procedure, precedent and legal jargon for which I was poorly equipped.

I had secured myself an alternative career in the Department of the Environment based in central Bristol, purely and simply because my parents lived nearby and I could commute daily. I was in charge of the riveting subject of town and country planning legislation for the south west of England. Oh yes, and I was also nominally in charge of Stonehenge!

Training for the role was less than adequate and I went to ask when I might be given some training to make me a more efficient civil servant. The local head of department seemed rather flummoxed by my enquiry. "But Mr Sadler you have a degree in geography" he said. I replied that was true, but explained I knew a lot about irrigation in central India but absolutely nothing about compulsory purchases of land and homes in Cornwall. He suggested a course *might* be forthcoming in perhaps November, some six months away and handed me a copy of the full Town and Country Planning Act 1972 by way of consolation.

In as polite a way as possible, bearing in mind I had only been there eight weeks, I thanked him and said I would be handing in my notice in the morning if that was all the Home Civil service could offer me.

With hindsight, a few unconnected incidents probably led me to my next career choice; my third in just nine months. My office, on the fourteenth floor of an office block, overlooked the rear yard of a busy central Bristol police station. Each time the two-tone horns sounded I was glancing out of the window onto a world which looked so much more exciting than my tedious In-tray / Out-tray job.

At that time I owned a lovely little blue MG Midget. This car had accompanied me to and back from the Isle of Man. The significance of this will soon become apparent.

After seven years of living independently, I was now living back home with my parents for a while. I was 24 years of age; bear this fact in mind in a moment.

I had owned the MG for about two years and for much of that time I'd had problems getting the twin carburetors to balance. I had just joined an MG owners club and one evening went to my first meeting in Bristol, telling my parents not to wait up for me. Remember, I am twenty four years of age and this was before the era of mobile phones.

The meeting went well and a fellow member offered to balance the carburetors for me. We drove back to his workshop after the meeting and I became so engrossed I didn't realise the clock had ticked past midnight. There I was driving back to Weston Super Mare where my parents lived at 12.30 am so not too late. I was about six miles from home when I became aware of flashing blue lights coming up quite fast behind me. A police car overtook me, drew in front and put on its "Stop" sign.

I pulled over and two burly officers got out and walked, oh-so-slowly, back towards me. I wound down the window to greet them. "Good evening sir" said the first officer in a rich Bristolian accent. "Are you Mr Sadler?" "Yes" I said."Mr Neil Sadler?" he said. Again I replied "Yes....is there a problem officer?"

"Well sir" he continued and it was so obvious he was trying his hardest not to laugh. "I don't fancy being in your shoes when you get home, sir". Mystified, I said, "Why is that officer?" "Well, your mother is really worried about you. She's called us to check if there have been any crashes tonight. And now she has reported you as *a missing person*!" As he turned away he carried on "Good night, sir...and good luck!"

And with that both officers hurried back to their patrol car with their shoulders rising up and down with laughter. I won't repeat what was said when I got home. Suffice to say, I was rather annoyed. But then again, I was an only child! But I must have sub consciously thought, there's a job where you could have some fun.

The other incident was rather more serious, but also had its comical side.

On the 10th December 1974 I was doing some harmless Christmas shopping with my girlfriend at the time, Norma. I was a student teacher and had a bedsitting room in the famous Great Pultney Street, Bath. You may recall the early to mid 1970s when the IRA bombing activity was at its peak on mainland Britain.

The Corridor in Bath is one of the world's earliest retail arcades, built in 1825. It followed the trend set by London's famous Burlington Arcade and was Grade II listed with a very attractive glass roof & marble columns.

This was the day the IRA decided to detonate one of their many bombs aimed at civilian targets in the UK. The subsequent blast from the 5lb bomb caused huge damage and forced the Corridor to undergo a major renovation programme. Bath isn't that big a city and we had walked along The Corridor a few times that day, but luckily not at the moment the explosives were detonated.

One of the first things the police did after the explosion and after the dust had (quite literally) settled, was to put out a radio and TV announcement. Remember this was a long time before the advent of CCTV.

This appeal was aimed at anyone who had taken photographs in the city that day.

They offered to develop and print people's films for free in return for allowing the photos to be viewed for clues, suspects etc. Unknown to me, Norma had heard this appeal and remembered she had snapped a few pictures while we had been out shopping. She dutifully went to the police station and handed in her camera.

A very short time later she was contacted and asked to return to the police station urgently. One of her developed photographs was of particular interest they told her. It showed a fantastic view of the still intact Corridor arcade with their prime suspect in a prominent position.

- The suspect was about 5'8" tall;
- He was wearing a green army combat jacket and jeans
- He had longish dark hair and a full beard
- Most significantly, he was holding a box under his arm and was standing only feet away from where the bomb had exploded.

Norma took one look at the photo and, with a wry smile said, "I'm afraid he's not an Irish terrorist, officer. He's actually my boyfriend and his name is Neil Sadler" So, for a short time in the mid-1970s I was in danger of being arrested as a potential IRA bomber.

Back to how I entered my third career in the space of a few months. From my desk in Bristol I telephoned Sussex police HQ to ask a very important question. Do you accept male recruits who have a beard? I knew that forces like Lancashire, Dorset and even the City of London would not allow me to join unless I shaved off my beard, something I had cultivated since the age of nineteen and was not going to do willingly.

The lady in the Recruiting department was quite shocked at my innocent question. "Of course we do dear, who doesn't?" So I reeled off my list of counties who had refused to accept me without the removal of my facial hair. Her next response has stayed with me for over forty years. "To be honest dear, we take anyone: when can you start?"

Fast forward four months, a ten week stint of basic training at the Police Training Centre in Ashford, Kent and I was ready to fight crime. Sussex here I come.

Middle row, fourth from the right.

The only officer with a full beard!

Chapter 3

First arrest and valuable lessons learned

I was without doubt quite naïve even at twenty four years of age. I had led a relatively sheltered life, growing up on the edge of Dartmoor. I attended a "nice school" and then went onto a teacher training college in the 1970s. I tended to believe what people told me; a principle not always healthy for a young police officer.

My first posting as a probationer constable was to the pleasures of Bognor Regis in November 1978. Bognor has few claims to fame apart from staging the annual Bird-Man event where slightly deranged people jump off the pier with wings strapped to their arms and "fly" into the sea. It's all for charity.

The late King George V is reputed to have said a very unkind thing about the town. This is a myth based on the fact that the King spent much time recuperating in Bognor Regis, which was a popular seaside resort even then. The story goes that on his deathbed the King was told, in an attempt to revive his spirits, "In no time at all you will be enjoying yourself in Bognor." To which George is said to have responded, "Bugger Bognor". These turned out to be his last words. The story, although amusing, was fairly rapidly debunked.

The town also has a huge Butlins holiday camp which supplied many "customers" in the summer holiday season, as some of the staff in those days were either career criminals or were actually wanted for offences.

I often talked about my first posting to Bognor Regis and how *some* of the staff at Butlins holiday camp were a bit on the rough side and how some were actually wanted by police forces in other parts of the UK, at times for quite serious offences.

23

At one particular talk on the south coast I had mentioned that some of the staff I met had just come out of prison (which was true). They had applied for a job at the holiday camp as it included a bed and board arrangement. Some were tattooed and pierced and wore broken noses almost as a badge of honour.

Talks experience: While packing away my equipment at the end of this talk, I was aware of a man standing right behind me. Without introduction he said "Actually I used to work at Butlins....***and*** I've got tattoos ***and*** a piercing......***and*** I have been arrested for GBH !!"

He then went on to point out a woman in the audience. He said that one evening he was in a pub in Rottingdean, near Brighton, when he saw a man come in, walk over to that woman and hit her in the face. At that point he said he ran over to this man and, in his words "smacked him on the nose", splitting it open because he was wearing three heavy gold sovereign rings on his fingers. When he appeared at court he was fined and ordered to pay £50 compensation to the man who had assaulted the female in the pub that night. Our knight in shining armour told the judge he would pay the fine but refused point blank to pay the other man a penny and asked what would happen if he didn't. The magistrate replied "I will have no choice but to imprison you", but our man could tell he was saying this reluctantly.

The JP apparently asked the clerk what time it was. He was told 2.15pm. "In that case" said the magistrate "I am imprisoning you until 4.30pm this afternoon......Case dismissed"

On my first day shift patrolling alone I remember stopping a young lad cycling the wrong way up a one way street in Bognor Regis. This was not the crime of the century, but I told him I'd need to speak to his parents.

He gave me his name and address and I dutifully wrote it down in my brand new, shiny pocket notebook. That evening, as promised, I popped around to the lad's address, only to find a retired couple living there who most certainly didn't have a 15 year old son with a bike

Rule number one: Do not always believe everything people tell you. I was astounded that a young lad would dare to lie to a policeman.

The following week I was on a full set of seven night shifts, working from 10pm to 6am. As you might imagine, Bognor is a fairly quiet place in the middle of the night in a bleak mid-November.

At about 3am I was walking in the High Street when I heard the loud smashing of breaking glass. I hurried around the corner to find a large window completely shattered and a solitary brick lying on the floor inside the travel agents shop. Why anyone would want to break into such a shop at 3am was beyond me and I looked up and down the road, but could see and hear no one running away. Neither was there anyone inside the shop attempting to pick up a glossy holiday brochure.

However, just beyond the travel agents were the main public toilets for the town car park. Perhaps someone had run in there before I came around the corner? For some unfathomable reason I wandered into the ladies loo first. I checked each cubicle; all clear. Then into the gents toilets.

No one there in the main area. However, as I peered under the door of the last cubicle, which was actually locked, I could see a pair of black shoes. The feet were facing away from the door, as if holding it closed. I removed my truncheon and did what I had always wanted to do; bang loudly on the door and announced in my most official voice "Police...open the door".

Slowly the door was opened and a short, middle aged man with a pencil moustache and greasy black hair appeared. The man wore a really heavy winter coat and was carrying a cardboard box under one arm. "Hello" I said as one does when meeting a stranger in a public toilet at 3am. "There's been a window broken at the travel agents next door. I don't suppose you saw anyone running away or driving away before you came in the loo?".

"No" he replied, "I only came in here to get warm about twenty minutes ago". Being the trusting young officer I was, I said thank you and started to walk away. I reached the main door of the toilet block when I heard footsteps running after me. "I did it. I smashed the window with a brick" said the man as he joined me outside. I was staggered. This man had run after me to admit to a crime.

He carried on in a rather sad voice." I've just been released from Ford Open prison this afternoon. I'm making my way towards Portsmouth, but I haven't got very far, have I? Maybe you had better take me in for the night, officer," and he thrust his hands forward, ready for the hand cuffs.

I really don't know who was more surprised; me that he had actually admitted to a crime or him that this wet-behind-the–ears copper had actually believed his initial cock and bull story.

This further consolidated my first lesson about people; don't always believe the first thing they tell you. Needless to say, this never happened to me again in the whole of the next thirty years police service. Maybe I should have retired that night.

I will deal with prisons and some of the characters I discovered in various prisons in a later chapter.

Bognor Regis, November 1978.

I am the officer on the left by the way.

Talks experience During my talks I would always illustrate how I banged on the toilet door by picking up my wooden truncheon, circa 1978, and rapping it loudly on the table. Unfortunately, I did this on one very sunny afternoon at a care home in Surrey. The residents appeared to be enjoying my ramblings, especially as the room was lovely and warm and they had just finished a filling lunch.

As I hit my truncheon on the table a lady on the front row shot to her feet and ran out of the room in front of me (narrowly missing my projector) and disappeared through the door, closely followed by a carer.

Rather taken aback, I just stopped mid-sentence. A short time later the two women reappeared and the carer settled the elderly lady back into her armchair. I asked if everything was alright.

"Well dear" explained the carer. "Mrs Smith had fallen asleep and when she heard you banging on the table she thought there was someone at the front door and rushed off to let them in."

After that experience I always tried to check that no one had nodded off before I used the same truncheon trick.

A number of other incidents in those first couple of years on the beat have had a profound effect on me. For the majority of the time police work is not quite like an episode of The Sweeney, The Bill or even Midsomer Murders.

No case is ever solved within the sixty minute time frame of a television programme. Every police officer will have examples of where they have come into contact with members of society who could be categorized as either "sad" or "bad". The following incidents stick in my mind, even after all these years.

One night shift my patrol car partner, John and I were called to a very nice house on a private estate on the outskirts of Bognor Regis. It seemed the owner of the house had been harassing her neighbours, including emptying her cat litter tray through their letter boxes; not very pleasant.

When the elderly lady let us into her house we noticed that every wall had been scribbled over with felt tip pen. Initially she seemed quite calm and lucid. It transpired she had worked in the Diplomatic Corps with a very high-powered job in the British Embassy in Tokyo, but had long since retired.

My colleague was talking to her and I was standing behind her when suddenly I coughed. She wheeled around and shouted at me saying I shouldn't laugh at her behind her back and that everyone had it in for her. This really took us both by surprise. However, we managed to calm the situation and left the house intending to do some follow up enquiries and inform Social Services in the morning as it was by then in the early hours.

Some hours later at about 4am, we received another call telling us that a postman on his way to work had noticed an elderly woman in a telephone kiosk. What was unusual was that she was totally naked. This was the middle of the night in early February.

John and I put two and two together and as it turned out, we were correct. It was our Diplomatic Corps lady again. She was indeed totally naked and shivering when we approached the telephone kiosk. I put a blanket around her and coaxed her back to the warmth of our patrol car. As I sat on the back seat with her, John began to drive away. Totally unexpectedly, the woman started to froth at the lips. Her eyes began to bulge wildly and she started to lunge towards me, trying to bite at my neck.

I tried to restrain her but she was unbelievably strong and aggressive for a seventy year old woman. I shouted at John to put his foot down and take us to Graylingwell Hospital in Chichester.

This was our nearest psychiatric hospital (this only closed in 2003). Formerly, it had been the West Sussex County Asylum, opened in 1897.

I had quite a struggle on the back seat, keeping her teeth away from my neck or any other part of me. I can still hear her howls and cries as the nursing staff carried her, struggling, down those long, Victorian corridors. But yet another important lesson had been learned that night. Never assume anything about someone just by their appearance. I will come back to that statement in a later chapter.

One afternoon in 1979 I was happily going about my foot patrol in Bognor Regis town centre when I received a call to a house. A woman had been making phone calls to a relative in Cambridgeshire. She had apparently told them she was (quote) "Covered in blood and in a state!"

There was no reply at the front door of the house, so I walked around to the back of the house and peered through the kitchen window. I could just make out a middle-aged woman lying on the kitchen floor apparently unconscious with her wrists lacerated and cuts to her stomach and groin. I could also see a blood-stained carving knife lying on the floor nearby.

Luckily, the back door was unlocked. I looked about the kitchen and used lots of tea towels to stem the bleeding while calling for an ambulance to come as soon as possible.

The lady then regained consciousness and started to become quite violent, attempting to pull my temporary bandages away from her wounds.

Suddenly, a man wandered into the kitchen from another part of the house. I assumed he was the woman's husband. He took one look at the blood spattered walls and floors and uttered words I shall never forget;

"What the hell has she done now. Look at these walls, I have only just finished decorating the bloody kitchen!" Rather than try and help, he just walked off making no attempt to assist either me or his critically injured wife. Luckily the ambulance crew arrived, sedated the woman and took her off to hospital.

Only a matter of weeks later the same woman made another attempt on her life and wandered onto the end of Bognor Regis pier in rough seas.

The local newspaper reported the incident under the headline "Police heroes in pier drama". "Two Bognor Regis policemen braved raging seas and high winds to haul a woman to safety from the end of the pier on Saturday afternoon"

It transpired the lady had walked across four-inch wide, slime covered girders above the foaming sea. She was found sitting with her legs dangling over the drop. The officers held onto her while she struggled. Eventually, a rescue helicopter winched all three off the pier and the woman was taken to hospital in Chichester.

One of the things a police officer must guard against is jumping to false assumptions based on appearances, what a person looks like, what they are wearing etc. It's an easy but dangerous trap to fall into. I have personally been a victim of this kind of dangerous stereotyping, prior to joining Sussex Police I must add.

Cast your mind back to that really hot summer of 1976. I had graduated that summer and decided to try my hand at hitch-hiking down through France and into northern Spain. On my way home the cross-channel ferries were on strike. My only way back to England was via Jersey. I managed to buy a ticket from the French channel port to St Helier.

In those days I had a full head of fairly long hair (happy days) and a straggly beard. I was carrying a rucksack, wearing a cheese-cloth shirt and (maybe) had not been able to have a good shower for a few days.

As I walked up the gang plank from the ferry onto Jersey, a couple of men in smart suits approached and asked me to accompany them to a nearby office. They made it pretty clear that I didn't have much choice. They introduced themselves as States of Jersey Police officers and asked how long I intended staying on _their_ island. I said something like as little time as possible as I had a friend's wedding to attend in Wiltshire. To this day I remember clearly the older officer saying: "Good. We don't have room for your sort on our island".

As you might imagine, I was rather taken aback (not to say offended) and told them I had just qualified as a school teacher and had a job lined up on the Isle of Man, where I hoped the local police might be less prone to stereotyping people on appearance.

Luckily, I got away with my cheek and they made sure I was on the next vessel to leave "their island". But it's been a lesson that has stayed with me since 1976 and served me well as a police officer.

Finally, there have been many occasions where funny moments have made the 30 years of dealing with the less savoury characters in our society worthwhile.

- The drunks who always want to shake your hand on a Saturday night outside the burger van;

- The inebriated girls on a hen night who want to try on your pointed helmet for size;

- The fancy dress party goers at a local Sussex country club who were so impressed with my *"realistic outfit"* when I visited to complete a licencing check one night. One person even asked me for the address of the costume hire company.

- Then there was the inept burglar in the park kiosk in the dead of night who kept handing out boxes of cigarettes to me, totally oblivious to the fact I was not actually his accomplice who had already been arrested. I know it was dark, but I thought the uniform might have given it away.

- The elderly lady who had just bought her first brand new automatic Mini Metro. She pushed her foot down hard on the wrong pedal, shot across the road, hit the kerb and catapulted straight through the window of the local cake shop. Her engine was still revving when I gently opened the car door and turned the ignition key off, then helped her out of the now wrecked car. I asked her what had happened and why she had decided to park actually inside the bakers shop, rather than parking on the road outside on the road like everyone else (well, maybe I have just made that bit up!) Bear in mind this was her first automatic car. As she went to pull away from the dealership's forecourt, she became confused and pressed down hard on the wrong pedal. Luckily, no one was injured, but there were a lot of really nice, cheap cakes to be had that day in Bognor Regis.

An incident straight out of Dad's Army happened to me in the summer of 1979. Whilst Bognor Regis is a typical south coast "kiss me quick" resort, the town has a number of very nice private estates on its outskirts. Places like the Craigwell and Aldwick Bay estates have houses which can boast direct access to the beach and seven figure prices to go with it.

A local estate agent was advertising such a property in 2018 with the following tempting information:

> *"A cottage once owned by Prince Harry's grandfather has gone on the market for £1.3million - and the owners have revealed childhood pictures of the royal were found in the next-door neighbour's loft.*
> *Princess Diana's father Earl Spencer previously lived in the striking seaside property in the West Sussex resort of Bognor Regis, which was last sold in 1994".*

It was to this Aldwick Bay estate that I was sent one quiet Sunday afternoon. There had been a spate of day time burglaries in the area and, as the youngest (and supposedly fittest) member of the section, it was thought I would be ideally suited to the task of maintaining observations.

I was expected to climb a large oak tree standing in the centre of a roundabout which commanded an excellent view of the main entrance to the estate.

I was wearing a green camouflage coat and very hot, green over-trousers. I had an ear piece connected to my police radio and a note pad to jot down details of any suspicious vehicles.

After about an hour of very limited activity, I saw a man leading a rather large Alsatian dog towards my grassy location. The dog took a keen interest in my tree, stood beneath it, cocked its leg and began to bark vigorously, all the while staring up at me. Luckily, I was well out of his reach. After about five minutes I was thankful when the man and his dog left the area as it wasn't exactly conducive to my covert observations.

A short while later my radio crackled into life. "Any unit available for the Aldwick Bay estate. A dog walker has reported a weird man squatting up a tree!" Neighbourhood Watch was alive and well in that area!

A colleague recalls another incident involving the house belonging to the father of Dianna Spencer on the same estate.

Two PCs were sent to an alarm at this rather prestigious property. They came back and told their sergeant the Princess of Wales came down in her dressing gown to make them tea. They didn't think anyone would believe them but by midday they were woken up by their irate Superintendent admonishing them in no uncertain terms.

Apparently, he had openly criticized the Royalty Protection Squad for not telling him she was resident in his sub division. They gently informed him that she was in fact safe and sound at Sandringham and he should really check his sources before sounding off!

Chapter 4

The Police Staff College, Bramshill: welcome to the House of Fun

The Royal Military Academy Sandhurst is the British Army's initial officer training centre. It's stated aim is to be "the national centre of excellence for leadership". All British Army officers, as well as other men and women from overseas, are trained at The Academy. The Royal Navy has Britannia Royal Naval College at Dartmouth and the Royal Air Force College is located at Cranwell in Lincolnshire.

For many years the training of senior police officers was organised in a somewhat piecemeal manner. Senior officers joined as constables and rose through the ranks. However, after World War Two, the need for a training college for the police service was pushed heavily by Sir Frank Newsam. He just happened to be the second most senior Home Office civil servant in the immediate post-war years.

Newsam got his way and the National Police College was established in June 1948. From 1948 to 1960 it was located at Ryton-on-Dunsmore, Warwickshire. However, it was felt a more prestigious location was required and, when Newsam became Permanent Secretary of the Home Office, he secured for it a rather prestigious home in Bramshill House, Hampshire, to which it moved in 1960.

Bramshill House is a magnificent building and is one of the largest and most important Jacobean mansions in England. It is also believed to be one of the most haunted houses in the country. Among the fourteen ghosts reputed to haunt the house is that of a bride who accidentally locked herself in a chest on her wedding night and was not found until 50 years later.

So impressive is the building and deer filled estate around it that Hermann Göering, architect of the Nazi police state in Germany, had insisted the site was never attacked. He intended to make it his home after the invasion of Britain. Luckily, he never moved in as he was condemned to hang as a war criminal by the International Military Tribunal at Nuremberg in 1946. He cheated the hangman, as he took poison instead and died the night his execution was ordered.

Now, I am giving this rather potted history lesson for a reason. Between January and December 1982 I was a resident student on what was known as the *"20th Special Course"* at Bramshill. I had joined Sussex police on the 4th September 1978 as a regular entrant. I possessed a degree but was only vaguely aware of an accelerated promotion system and, as I got married shortly after joining, I had no desire to leave my new bride for a protracted period of training.

Unfortunately, my superintendent at Bognor Regis had other ideas. Bill Roberts had himself been a product of one of the very first "Special courses" and seemed to take an interest in my career. He suggested I might like to apply for accelerated promotion, although all I really wanted to do was get established in my new job, for Julie and me to decorate our police house and buy our first dog together!

Fate took a hand when I passed the sergeants' exam in the top 200 in the country and could automatically apply for the course. I approached my application with luke-warm enthusiasm, not least because it seemed a daunting process. I was going to face three gruelling days of assessments.

Day one consisted of group discussions and written appreciation tests. The pace was upped on day two with intelligence tests, drafting exercises and then interviews with service and non- service personnel. The latter, from memory, were civil servants and academic types.

As I walked into the interview for a 1:1 session with a professor from Newcastle university, the man stood up, walked towards the window, climbed onto the ledge and said "Right, that's it. I am going to kill myself". I stood there looking at him but making no sudden move to grab him. "Well what are you going to do then?" he demanded.

Having heard of these "wind-up" type activities, designed to test interviewees reactions to stress, I calmly said I was going to do nothing as he was quite clearly an intelligent person who had made his mind up. With that, the professor slammed the window shut, walked back to his side of the desk and said, "Right,that's the stupid stuff over, let's get on with the serious stuff".

Having consulted the faded programme which I have kept in my first scrap book, it seems the rest of the three days were taken up with yet more interviews, intelligence tests, a committee exercise and finally between 1230pm and 1235pm on the last day a session called "mutual ranking". Goodness only knows what that session was all about, but it can't have taken very long.

I have scribbled in pen on my programme "1.30pm train to London" as the procedure had taken place at the Derbyshire police HQ at Butterley Hall, near Ripley. No doubt a huge sigh escaped my lips as I got onto that train.

Of all the things that happened over those taxing three days, what I remember most is that the waitresses in the officer's mess had to wear white gloves whilst serving our meals. I will never forget the lady approaching my table with a tureen of tomato soup. As she neared me she tripped slightly and the red soup slopped up her fingers. "Oh bugger" she exclaimed in a very loud Derbyshire accent to the great amusement of all of us in the room.

To this day I am absolutely convinced the only reason I was successful at the assessment centre was because I had approached it with a laissez-faire attitude. I didn't really want to attend the course it would lead to. That is not false modesty I assure you, but going away from home for a whole twelve months was the last thing I wanted to do. Also, if I am honest with myself, I didn't feel as intellectually gifted as most of the people I had met at Ripley.

To cut a very long story short, I was one of twenty two sergeants to attend the 20th Special Course in 1982. I won't pretend I enjoyed my time there, as it coincided with my wife giving birth to our first child, Rachael. Things often happen for a reason in my experience. One Wednesday afternoon in April 1982 I had agreed to play rugby for the Staff College team. After only twenty minutes I found myself in an ambulance on my way to Frimley Park hospital with internal injuries. My tip for any aspiring rugby players is not to lift your head up in a scrum if you are playing hooker just as the ball gets put in by the scrum half. Fifteen men then push as hard as they can; sadly, this was into my chest!

I had all sorts of tests and x- rays but, luckily, I had only sustained crushed ribs. As I lay in my hospital bed, the Chief Superintendent in charge of my course turned up for the obligatory welfare visit. He was a dapper, well-spoken man on secondment from Essex police who loved telling people he was also quite high up in the Territorial army and a fluent German speaker.

All I could hear was my nurse (who was German) gabbling on to the Chief Superintendent in the corridor. He spent a mere five minutes with me but told me I would be driven to join my pregnant wife who was soon to give birth and I would need a few weeks to recover.

Bearing in mind my ribs were heavily bandaged and I couldn't even cough gently without extreme pain, what happened next is not to be recommended. The nurse who had been conversing in the corridor suddenly appeared. *"Who vaz zat vanker who thinks he can speak German?"* she demanded. It took me ten minutes and quite a few pain killers to recover. The upside to all this is that I spent the next three weeks with Julie and new baby daughter, much to the envy of the two other new fathers on the course.

I hadn't really endeared myself to the German speaking head of the course. Some weeks before the unfortunate rugby injury the course made a visit to Heathrow police station to look at aviation security. Bearing in mind I had only just left a stint of wandering around Gatwick airport, I was probably not as enthusiastic as some of my colleagues.

We had endured a pretty dry briefing from the local commander and before we set off for a more detailed tour, I thought it advisable to nip to the loo. Another sergeant joined me and as we were standing there he was enthusing about how interesting the day had been so far. "Oh yes" I said in a sarcastic tone "It's just like school. They will have us writing about it and drawing bloody pictures next!"

At that very moment the chain flushed in one of the cubicles. Out walked the Chief Superintendent in charge of the course. "So that's what you think of my course is it Sergeant Sadler?" Whoops. After that I always checked there was no one in the cubicles before saying anything derogatory about anything.

My attendance on the Special Course guaranteed me promotion to the rank of Inspector. After twelve months as a patrol Sergeant I found myself as a new Inspector at Worthing in January 1984. This was after a mere five years service. Whilst I enjoyed the challenge, I never could shake off the thoughts of what I had missed out doing.

This included never getting the chance to drive the powerful traffic patrol cars, growing my hair and beard long and becoming a drugs squad officer or becoming a specialist in a particular field. I would frequently be the youngest Inspector at a police station and often much younger than most of the sergeants and constables whom I was expected to supervise, lead and mentor.

The purpose of the Special Course was to enable the service to produce its own leaders by giving early training to those who had displayed suitability for high rank. Back in 2012 a review was undertaken to see how effective this accelerated promotion scheme had been. Between 1962 and 1992 the scheme had produced 35 Chief Constables, 31 Deputy Chief Constables and 60 Assistant Chief Constables. A line in the report made me smile when it said;

> *"Fourteen per cent of the sample remained at the rank of Inspector, which demonstrates that not everyone who succeeds on such a scheme will progress as intended"* *

* Independent Review of Police Officer and Staff Remuneration.. Winsor, 2012

I was clearly one of those "disappointments" but, to be honest, I really didn't have the drive, determination or willingness to uproot my family to move around the country like others of my cohort.

Out of pure nosiness, I undertook a little research to see how successful the 20th Special Course had been. To my knowledge out of the twenty officers who completed the course (two Metropolitan officers were "returned to Force" part way through the year, but that is another story) at least six of my former colleagues had made it to Chief Constable. Most of these had also received a knighthood for their troubles. Another had become the Chief inspector of Prisons on his retirement from the Metropolitan police.

One had gone on to become the first ever Commissioner for Standards in the House of Lords having also been Chief Constable of Hampshire.

Interestingly, there had been five women Sergeants on my course. Despite some research, I could only find one who had achieved Chief Constable rank. She had then climbed the ladder even further and become an Inspector of Constabulary (HMIC). This organisation independently assesses police forces, asking the questions that citizens would ask and publishing information to allow the public to compare the performance of their force against others.

I so recall the day I went with this lady on a visit back to Derbyshire HQ in 1982 as lowly Sergeants. On our arrival we had been given identification badges and were shown into the Assistant Chief Constable's office. My colleague, Jane, had noticed her surname had been crossed through in pen and a new name inserted. When the rather suave senior officer joined us he approached Jane. "Ah, I see you have just had a happy event", he said assuming she had recently got married.

"Yes sir" said Jane trying to keep a straight face, "I've managed to get rid of him after all these years". She had, in fact, just become divorced. The senior officer went bright red and suggested it was time to start the meeting.

My abiding memory of my first day as a new Inspector with white shirt and shiny pips on my shoulder, was when I walked into the office shared with other Inspectors at Worthing police station. As I entered, I saw a row of lockers against a wall. Sitting with his back to me was an older man beavering away at a pile of paperwork. "Hello" I said "Can you tell me which is my locker please?"

Without even acknowledging me or turning around, the other man said, "Can't you tell? It's the one with the calendar on it with all the dates crossed off. Your predecessor couldn't wait to get out of here". Inspector Ted Street (RIP) was a man of few words!

Chapter 5

The rise of "Robo-cop": Changes in equipment and technology

I would always start my first Policeman's Lot talk with a clip of music. Not only did it cause a degree of surprise for the audience, but it also led nicely into my first story of why I had joined the police in 1978.

I would play the opening bars of the theme tune from the hit tv series Z Cars. For those too young to remember, I would explain it was a TV series centred on the work of uniformed police officers in the fictional northern town of Newtown. This was based on Kirby in Merseyside. It was produced by the BBC and began in January 1962 running until September 1978.

It wasn't universally popular at the time, as it injected a new element of harsh realism into the image of the police. Z-Cars ran for 803 episodes and launched many acting careers. Regular stars included: Stratford Johns, who played hard bitten Detective Inspector Barlow, James Ellis played Irishman Bert Lynch and who could forget Brian Blessed who portrayed PC "Fancy" Smith.

I used to explain that I had grown up in the 1950s and 60s and had watched Z cars morph from black and white to a full colour production. Coincidentally, the year and month it disappeared from our screens was the exact time I joined Sussex police and became a real officer.

So, back in the late 1970s what did I have to help me do the job and protect myself if called on to do so? So called PPE in pandemic jargon (personal protective equipment). In case I encountered extreme danger, I was given a fourteen inch piece of polished wood; a truncheon. Female officers' truncheons were even smaller, so they could be kept hidden in their black leather shoulder bags.

Mine slipped neatly (and rather uncomfortably) into a special silky little pocket in my trousers. This was something you had to remember when you started to run or attempted to climb over a wall, gate etc, especially if you fancied having children one day!

A friend of mine had the misfortune of dropping his truncheon onto the hard parade ground at initial training school; sadly for him, it shattered into three pieces, due to a bad case of woodworm.

Today officers carry an extending metal baton called an ASP. This opens with a deft flick of the wrist making a satisfying "crack" sound. As the company who markets them says:

 "ASP tactical batons work by using a friction lock system of telescopic tubes, which can be deployed almost instantly. Greater striking force is created and so officers are able to control violence with fewer strikes.". That's handy, especially if you are the person being hit!

The in-between stage in the early 1990s saw me carrying a Monadnock Side-Handled baton. This was incredibly long and cumbersome to put it mildly. We practised for hours on end, learning moves and blocks in the hope we would never need to use them! Unless you were sixteen feet tall, the side handled baton was never going to slide into your side pocket. Consequently they gave us a natty little plastic hoop which fitted on the equipment belt. The baton just dangled there like a sword.

Captor Spray : Today Sussex officers are equipped with a Captor Spray canister which is attached to their equipment belts. The main ingredient in Captor is a chemical used in pain relief creams. It is milder than CS spray and has no health risks but is more than 90% effective in incapacitating a really violent person. The spray projects a jet of liquid into a person's eyes and causes an immediate burning pain. All it requires is about a pin head of the stuff to make life very uncomfortable for the person sprayed.

You might say that because you wear spectacles you are not too worried. Well, the officer just needs to spray onto your eyebrows and the nasty liquid will drip down into one eye. Police officers have to demonstrate they were justified in using it to restrain a violent suspect. For some unknown reason, my daughter volunteered to have Captor sprayed into her eyes on a training day demonstration.

Her reaction afterwards said it all. "It's just like a burning feeling in my eyes - it's like they're on fire". It should stop someone from being aggressive, assaulting somebody and it also stops them from running off. The spray needs to be removed as soon as possible with water, usually at the cell block and after the detained person has calmed down. Should you have the misfortune to be squirted with Captor you are provided with an information sheet on your release. It makes for quite amusing reading, especially if like me you are not a big fan of curry.

And I quote: *There may be the following effects: This will cause discomfort to the eyes and a burning sensation to the skin. If you have swallowed any you should not experience any internal discomfort at all although your mouth will feel as though you have eaten very spicy food such as curry.*

Handcuffs: They have changed very little since I joined. However, I learnt a rather embarrassing lesson one night. After a late shift in Worthing in the mid 1980s I would travel home with my handcuffs in their case attached to my belt, just in case I saw something untoward on the journey.

This was in pre mobile telephone days and I never knew what I might come across late on a Friday or Saturday night.

This particular night I arrived home around 3 am and tried hard not to wake my wife and two slumbering daughters (our second child, Gilly had been born in 1984 and a few decades later she would follow me into Sussex Police). I left the bedroom light off but when I removed my trousers the handcuffs fell out of their pouch and crashed to the hard wood floor, making a terrible noise. My wife shot up in bed and I gingerly placed the offending items on a bedside cupboard. The next evening I went to work at 6pm and realized I had left the handcuffs at home. Without thinking, I called up on the police radio and asked if anyone was near my house. One officer said he was and did I want him to collect something? Again, without thinking, and so that everyone was able to hear, I asked him to go and see my wife and collect the handcuffs which were on the bedside cabinet.

You can imagine the howls of laughter this request caused at the thought of the Inspectors's wife going upstairs to collect her husband's handcuffs from the matrimonial bedroom. I don't know who was more embarrassed; my wife, the young constable or me.

Talks experience: At one regional Womens' Institute meeting. I was approached by a rather elderly, frail looking lady, of about eighty years of age. She leaned over to me and, in a conspiratorial whisper, said, "I wonder if you would do something for me before you leave today, dear? I replied that it very much depended on what she had in mind. She then said "Well, will you handcuff me before you leave, as I have always wondered what it felt like". As if that wasn't weird enough, she carried on "But you will have to be very careful, as I bruise easily these days". I said she might have been reading too many of those racy, Fifty shades of Grey type books. I conveniently forgot about this request and left the meeting fairly swiftly after the talk.

Whilst we are still on the subject of handcuffs; did you know the Spanish word for them is *esposas*. By an amazing coincidence the Spanish word for wife or bride happens to be *esposa*.

Taser: A Taser is an electro-shock weapon that can stun a subject by firing electrodes on the end of long thin wires. Their effective distance is around ten feet. Tasers were introduced as non-lethal weapons to be used by police to subdue fleeing, belligerent, or potentially dangerous subjects. They could be used instead of more lethal weapons which may have been deployed in the past, such as Heckler and Koch machine gun.

The Taser fires two small dart-like electrodes, which stay connected to the main unit by conductive wires. They are propelled by small compressed nitrogen charges similar to some air guns and an electrical charge passes down them. Someone struck by a Taser experiences stimulation of their sensory nerves resulting in strong involuntary muscle contractions. They create a 50,000 volt charge causing the target to lose muscle control and collapse.

The headline : *Gatwick police Taser gunman in front of terrified passengers,* appeared in the Daily Mail in July 2009. This was one of the first times a Taser had been discharged in Sussex. The accompanying article said a man had been spotted with a handgun as he got off a bus at the airport's South Terminal. Officers used the 50,000-volt stun gun to disarm him in front of holidaymakers checking in for their flights. The man had been challenged by police before he was stunned and arrested.

Spit hoods. According to Wikipedia *"A spit hood, spit mask, or spit guard is a restraint device intended to prevent someone from spitting or biting."*

Proponents, including police unions, say spit hoods can help protect personnel from exposure to serious infections like hepatitis. My

48

daughter, Gilly, was issued with such a device and carried it on her equipment belt at all times.

Even working in semi-rural, mid-Sussex she was forced to use one on a number of occasions on women, as well as men. When arrested and handcuffed a prisoner can't hit you. If they are placed in the rear seat of a patrol car, they can't kick you. However, they can still spit at you; a most revolting practice. As a result, Sussex police decided to issue all uniform patrol officers with protective hoods.

During the corona virus pandemic in 2020 dreadful stories emerged of some people "weaponizing" the act of spitting at key workers such as police officers, nurses and ambulance crews.

Gilly gave me an old spit hood and I would end my first police talk by placing the mesh over my head (after remembering to remove my spectacles, which was something I failed to do the first time) I would then ask the group to guess what this particular piece of police equipment was used for.

I would tell them it wasn't to preserve a persons' identity, nor was it to protect officers from a swarm of angry bees. I also mentioned there was a small prize for the person who guessed correctly. This was partly a selfish move on my part, as wearing the hood is a less than pleasant experience. The sooner I got an answer, the sooner it was whipped off my head.

Talks experience The very first time I used this trick was at a church group in Haywards Heath. Almost as soon as I had donned the hood a woman in the front row called out loudly "That's a spit hood to stop prisoners spitting at you"

I was surprised she had guessed so quickly and, without thinking, quipped. "Well it's a well- known fact that people who guess so quickly have probably been arrested themselves". The audience roared, but the lady who had guessed just glared at me

---

I turned to start packing my equipment away and became aware of someone standing immediately behind me.

It was the lady who had made the correct guess. In a very severe voice and still wearing a glare she demanded,

"Tea of Coffee?"

I replied "Tea, no sugar thanks" and carried on moving my props.

"And another thing, young man," the woman continued, her voice rising an octave, " I have _never_ been arrested in my life. I am _actually_ a magistrate!" At which point she stormed off.

I then realised why all her friends had reacted the way they had when I accused her of having been arrested.

They knew she was a magistrate but I didn't!

I have frequently been asked the same question at police talks. "Would you join the police again knowing what you know now?"

It is a very difficult question to answer because forty years ago society and the environment in which I was working was so different from today. I have explained about the various items of personal safety equipment issued to officers in 2020. This has changed due to the nature of the role and the threat level to officers' safety.

The other aspect which is different is the authorized officer establishment. When I retired in 2008 there were 142,342 warranted police officers (those with powers to arrest) in England and Wales. This compares with 124,784 police officers in England and Wales at 30 September 2019 (_source Office of National Statistics; Home Office Statistical bulletin 02/20_)

The demands handled by police forces have also changed dramatically since 2010 when serious cuts to all public services began. We have seen rising cybercrime, fraud, investigations into historical sex offences, not to mention a newly disclosed phenomenon of "modern slavery". As other agencies have pulled back through austerity, the police service has ended up picking up some of the pieces. Many officers today see the job as more akin to social services work rather than law enforcement and crime reduction.

Boris Johnson made a pledge in his first speech as prime minister in 2019, vowing outside 10 Downing Street that he would "make your streets safer".

He announced an increase in police numbers by 20,000, but analysis by The Independent suggested that more than 46,000 would have to be hired to meet that target and also replace officers leaving the service over the following three years.

In my personal opinion the removal of the "village bobby" has had an adverse effect on local community engagement and feelings of security. In 1986 I was the rural section Inspector covering the whole of mid-Sussex.
This is a huge geographical area from south of Crawley down to Pyecombe, which borders the city of Brighton and Hove. Working with me at that time were two Sergeants and twelve Constables, the majority of whom lived in their respective village police houses. Most had been in post for a considerable time and knew their "beat" well and the people who lived there. Equally importantly, they could recognise the stranger, the unusual van or car and were fully aware of crime patterns in their area.

One incident exemplifies this situation perfectly. I had just started my new role and was keen to meet my officers "in situ". The first place I went to was Handcross to the far north of the division. There I met the village constable and, after introducing myself, I suggested he showed me around his large rural patch.

We hadn't driven more than a hundred yards when he said "See that man on the left, Guv, he's a well known burglar". We passed a man getting into a battered old van. "See that bloke. He's a poacher". A matter of minutes later I noticed a woman coming out of the post office. "See that woman. She's having an affair with the post man".

With the closure and sale of all the rural police houses that accumulated local knowledge has disappeared. Sadly, I think it will be too expensive to ever get it back.

Chapter 6

Missing person searches.

A great deal of police time is taken up with dealing with reports of missing people, or as they are known for short, "mispers".

People can go missing for a host of different reasons:

- Because they suffer from dementia or memory loss and genuinely don't know what they are doing;
- They run away deliberately; for instance, to escape from a violent relationship or to leave their debts and worries behind temporarily.

Sometimes and very, very occasionally they are abducted, such as little Sarah Payne who disappeared on 1st July 2000 from a cornfield near the home of her grandparents in Kingston Gorse, near Littlehampton, in West Sussex.

Sarah, aged nine, had been playing in a field with her brothers and sister at the time. A nationwide search began and Sarah's parents made many television appeals for her safe return.

On 17 July, a body was found in a field near Pulborough, some 15 miles from where she had disappeared. Subsequently a local man, Roy Whiting, was questioned about the disappearance, which had taken place about 5 miles from where Whiting lived.

One of Sarah's shoes was found by a member of the public in a country lane and forensic tests found fibres from Roy Whiting's van on the shoe. This was the only item of Sarah's clothing to be recovered. A strand of blonde hair on a T-shirt was found in Whiting's van. DNA testing established there was a one-in-a-billion chance of it belonging to anyone other than Sarah Payne.

On 12 December 2001, after a four week trial, Whiting was convicted of the abduction and murder of Sarah and sentenced to life imprisonment. This case was notable for the extensive use of various forensic sciences in establishing the prosecution case against Whiting. Twenty forensic experts from a variety of disciplines were employed during the inquiry, including entomology, pathology, geology and archaeology. The investigation had involved one thousand personnel and cost more than £2 million. However, many misper enquiries have a happier ending.

My first involvement in a high profile "misper" enquiry was on a sunny day in the summer of 1980. On Friday 8th August, a two year old girl called Elizabeth Peck had been playing hide and seek with her sisters during a family picnic on the edge of Houghton Forest, on the South Downs, above Arundel.

Somehow, she managed to wander off into the dense forest and her parents started to search for her, but in vain. You can only imagine how frantic they must have felt. A massive police search operation began and over the whole of that weekend 700 volunteers and 140 officers undertook a huge search.

Now it is commendable that so many people turned out on that summer to help with the search. However, it is not unreasonable to expect people to follow instructions when assisting the police effort. Some searchers thought they knew better than us and wandered off independently into remote areas of the forest; only to get lost themselves and then expected us to find *them*.

In addition, others wandered off in a direction we had specifically cautioned against. One or two tripped over in the dense woodland, injured themselves and had the nerve to lodge a claim for damages against Sussex police on the following Monday morning.

I was transported daily from Bognor Regis and we set about searching pre-determined areas where it was likely a two year old could reach. Whilst there was absolutely no evidence Elizabeth had been abducted, rather than just wandering off, that was always another line of enquiry.

Finally, on the Sunday morning, forty hours after she had last been seen, one of the many volunteers spotted a small bundle moving in the dark woods. This location was some 2 ½ miles from her point of disappearance. They had found Elizabeth Peck.

The little girl was taken to St Richards Hospital, Chichester and, although rather dehydrated and very hungry, she amazed the doctors as she only had a spot of nappy rash and a few scratches

As her mother said in the Daily Mail a day or two later; *"I must admit we didn't think we would get her back alive after two nights out in the open."*

I have been trying to locate Elizabeth for many years, as I still have the press cuttings relating to this incident which even featured on national tv news programmes. I would love to ask her if she had children of her own now and, if she did, whether she lets them play hide and seek in the woods!

The newspaper report at the time had said her parents, Robin and Christine Peck, lived in Lowden Road, Brixton. They had been told of their daughter's discovery as they returned from church after praying for her.

In 2018 I really thought I had succeeded in my search. I read in a newspaper article that the leader of Lambeth council had the name of *Lib Peck,* but her official name was Elizabeth. I quickly dashed off an email to the council.

It read as follows;

> *Hello I wonder if you can assist me please?*
>
> *I am a retired Sussex police officer who gives talks / presentations across the South East. One of my cases relates to the successful 48 hour search for a young girl in 1980 called Elizabeth Peck, whom I believe came from Lowden Rd in Brixton.*
>
> *Elizabeth had been with her family at Butlins in Bognor Regis and had wandered off into dense forest near Arundel. The search made national TV and newspapers (of which I have a copy). I just wondered if Ms Peck is that same person or if she actually knows the person involved, as I would love to know what became of her.*
>
> *Thank you for your time*

Within a few days I received the following reply from the PA to Councillor Lib Peck at the Leaders Office.

> *Dear Mr Sadler,*
> *Thank you for your enquiry but Cllr Peck has advised me that she was not the missing girl nor is she any relation. Sorry not to be able to assist but can we wish you the best of luck in your continuing search.*

The search had run cold. It turned out that Ms Peck had actually been born in 1967, so would have been thirteen years old in 1980, not two years of age.

> **Talks experience**   Some thirty eight years after the search for Elizabeth I was giving the Policeman's Lot talk at a Women's Institute meeting about four miles from where the search had taken place.
>
> When I showed a slide from the Daily Mail of the little girl in her mothers arms, under the title *"Lost Girl"* I noticed a woman on the front row visibly bristle and fold her arms defensively.
>
> I asked her, quite innocently, if she remembered this case. She replied "Yes I do" in a rather angry way, taking me by surprise. I asked her if there was a reason to remember it.
>
> She responded, "I remember it very well, as my husband was late for the birth of our first child as he was out looking for **her!**"

Another missing person case I have taken a close interest in relates to "drowned canoeist" John Darwin back in 2002. Darwin, of Seaton Carew, Teesside, faked his own death so his then-wife Anne could claim over half a million pounds in life insurance.

The background to this case is fascinating. John Darwin was reported missing whilst paddling a canoe in the North Sea in March 2002. His wife, Anne was well aware of the scam and while John hid in an adjacent house, the couple's two sons believed their father was dead. The couple subsequently fled to central America with their ill- gotten gains.

In December 2007, Darwin walked into a London police station, claiming to have amnesia. His wife, who had fled with him to Panama, pretended to be shocked until a photograph emerged of them posing together after his supposed death. She was later jailed for six-and-a-half years for fraud and money laundering.

57

After the pair were jailed, assets including an apartment in Panama City and an overgrown plot of land near the artificial Lake Gatun were seized and sold. The Crown Prosecution Service was granted a confiscation order to retrieve the money Anne Darwin received from the insurance companies and pension funds.

At a talk in Eastbourne, a lady approached me and spoke in a very broad Teeside accent. She asked me if I knew where the Darwins used to live.

I replied that it was a small seaside village called Seaton Carew. She said I was correct and that she had lived there herself and had actually known the infamous couple. She had only recently moved to Eastbourne on retirement.

I was fascinating and asked if I could buy her a cup of tea so she could tell me more about them. At the end of a fascinating conversation she said "Do you want to hear a funny story about them?" Naturally I said I did. She then told me that shortly after the couple were found guilty at Crown Court, some wag from the village removed the Welcome to Seaton Carew road sign. The person replaced it with a new sign on which was painted "Welcome to Seaton Canoe; twinned with Panama". Sadly, the local council were not amused and that sign was removed fairly swiftly.

In 2014 Teesside Crown Court ordered Darwin to pay back £40,000 in a lump sum from two matured pensions over the next year. The court heard divorced Darwin, who was now claiming benefits, had only paid back £121 of the money he had been told to repay at his original court case. At that time he had been ordered to repay £679,073, cheated out of insurance companies a decade before.

The former teacher and prison officer did not challenge the application by the Crown to have the £40,000 removed from his bank accounts which were the subject of restraints.

During my first Policeman's Lot talk I normally show a number of photographs of famous or infamous people. One is a black and white photograph of John Bingham, better known as the seventh Earl of Lucan.

He disappeared without trace early on 8 November 1974 after his estranged wife's nanny had been found murdered in London. He is believed to have driven to Uckfield in East Sussex to visit his friends, Ian and Susan Maxwell-Scott. The day after the murder a Ford Corsair car believed to have been driven from London by Bingham was discovered outside Newhaven ferry port. The assumption being that he had jumped on a ferry and escaped to France

Bingham was officially declared dead by the High Court in 1999. At one talk in Uckfield a lady called out "You know where he's buried, don't you dear". I said "Where's that then?" She replied "Under the local bowls club green".

Now, initially I thought she had something against the Uckfield Bowls Club, but someone else, on another occasion said the same thing, so I undertook some research. It turned out the house Lucan visited was called Grants Hill House and has since been demolished. Part of the garden of that house is now used by the town's bowls club

A BBC investigation in 2005 learned that a mystery man made several anonymous phone calls to Sussex police in May 1998. All were from the same man and repeated the same story. He alleged that Lucan had been shot and buried in the grounds of Grants Hill House on the night of his flight from London. The mystery caller claimed he had been in the grounds of the property that night and he had witnessed three people walking from the house towards the bottom of the garden. Taken by surprise, the caller said he retreated into the undergrowth where he heard two gun shots. He then heard a splash and two, not three, people walked back to the house.

Investigative journalists from the programme spoke with two police sources who confirmed the existence of the mystery caller, although they declined to be interviewed on camera. The witness (who one can only assume was in the grounds for nefarious purposes that night) claimed that Lucan must have been murdered and his body dumped in the cess pit in the grounds of the house.

Using old building plans, the reporters discovered there had been a cess pit in that approximate location. This is now under the beautifully manicured lawns of the Uckfield Bowls Club; hence the local tale about the dead aristocrat. Ironically, the club has a bar called, of all things, *"Lord Lucan's Tavern"*.

When discussing missing person reports and searches I would often ask if anyone remembered certain high-profile cases. One slide I would show was a photograph often used by the media of a little girl called Madelaine McCann. Maddy, as she was often known, had been abducted from the bedroom of a Portuguese holiday complex at Praia da Luz in May 2007.

It was surprising how many people had their own theories about what really happened to the poor little girl on that night. Her disappearance became the subject of intense international publicity, but no sign of her was ever found and the police in Portugal shelved their initial investigation in 2008.

However, in 2011, following a lengthy campaign by the McCann family, the Prime Minister, David Cameron, ordered a review of the case by Scotland Yard. Operation Grange was set up in 2013 to supplement the Portuguese efforts and continued to follow leads into her abduction. At its height there had been twenty nine officers working on the case in London but this was later scaled back to just four.

The out of date photograph of a very young Madelaine was soon "age-progressed" by Scotland Yard experts to show what she might look like as a teenager. Amazingly, when I was in Rye East Sussex back in 2015, I actually saw the more up to date photograph on a Missing Person poster in the local Post Office. It said something like;

"Are you going on holiday in Portugal, Spain or France? If so, please look out for a young girl who might look like this. It might be missing Madeleine McCann"

When I checked the current state of the investigation in late 2019, the Home Office website said the following about funding for the on-going operation; Last year (2018) the Home Office provided £300,000 of funding to the Metropolitan Police Service. The cost of Operation Grange to date is £11.75m.

> **Talks experience**. A lady came up to me after one talk and told me she had just sold her time share apartment on the Algarve in Portugal. She said "I suppose you want to know why". Of course, my curiosity had been piqued. She went on "I am fed up with being stopped in the street down there when I'm walking around with my grand daughter. She is a teenager and has long fair hair and keeps being mistaken for the missing Madeleine McCann"

On 3 December 1926, a Mr Archie Christie asked his wife, Agatha, for a divorce. He was in love with another woman called Nancy Neele. The pair quarreled, and Archie left their house, Styles, in Sunningdale, Berkshire, to spend the weekend with his mistress at Godalming in Surrey.

That evening, around 9:45 pm, well known author Agatha Christie disappeared from her home, leaving behind a letter for her secretary saying that she was going to Yorkshire. Her car, a Morris Cowley, was later found at Newlands Corner, not far from a lake near Guildford, Surrey with some clothes and an expired driving licence in her name.

Her disappearance caused an outcry from the public, as even then she was a celebrated writer. The Home Secretary of the day, William Joynson-Hicks, pressured police, and apparently ordered over a thousand police officers to assist in the search. Where do you get a thousand cops from these days? Fifteen thousand volunteers and several airplanes scoured the rural landscape. A newspaper even offered a £100 reward. Sir Arthur Conan Doyle gave a spirit medium one of Christie's gloves in the hope of finding the missing woman. Author Dorothy L Sayers visited the matrimonial home in Surrey, later using the scenario in her book Unnatural Death. Sayers is best known for her mysteries with a series of novels and short stories set between the First and Second World Wars, featuring English aristocrat and amateur sleuth Lord Peter Wimsey,

Christie's disappearance even featured on the front page of *The New York Times*. Despite the extensive manhunt, she was not discovered for ten days. On the 14th December, she was found at the Swan Hydropathic Hotel (now the Old Swan Hotel) in Harrogate, North Yorkshire, registered under the name of Mrs Teresa Neele from Cape Town. (you might recall her husband's lover was a Mrs Nancy Neele)

Christie's autobiography makes no reference to her disappearance. Although two doctors diagnosed her as suffering from amnesia, opinion remains divided as to why she disappeared. She was known to be in a depressed state from overwork, her mother's death earlier that year and her husband's infidelity. Public reaction at the time was largely negative, supposing it had all been a publicity stunt or an attempt to frame her husband for murder.

On a number of occasions at talks, I got myself into "hot water" by light heartedly saying "Of course none of you here today will have been around in 1926". Big mistake; some ladies were even older than they looked. One lady was presented after my talk with a magnificent stone bird bath to celebrate her 100th birthday that day.

My all-time favourite missing person story concerned a gentleman named Bernard Jordon. When I mentioned his name, no one ever remembered him. That was until I added that he had been the eighty-nine year old World War Two veteran who had walked out of his Hove care home in 2014 to join his old comrades on the Normandy landing beaches to commemorate those who didn't return, seventy years before.

Bernard had disappeared without saying where he was going at 1030am and the former mayor of Hove was reported to Sussex police as an official missing person later that day.

It transpired that staff at The Pines Nursing Home where he lived with his wife had tried to get Bernard on an accredited tour with the Royal British Legion. However, it had not been possible due to the last minute nature of the request. He had taken part in Operation Overlord as a Royal Navy officer. So, wearing a grey raincoat to hide the medals pinned to his best suit, he slipped out of the home, headed for Brighton station and caught a train to Portsmouth.

Showing all the determination that got him through the Normandy landings he then caught a ferry to France. After prompting an international missing persons alert, he joined hundreds of his friends to commemorate the heroism and sacrifice of those who did not survive the largest seaborne invasion in history. Happily, the Royal Navy veteran returned safely after meeting up with former colleagues. Sussex Police later said in a statement, "Once the pensioner is home, we will go and have a chat with him to check he is OK".

Bernard appeared on national TV news programmes. The Daily Telegraph cartoonist, Bob, even drew a fantastic colour picture which parodied the famous scene in the 1963 war film "The Great Escape". It showed Bernard, astride a motor bike, jumping over the barbed wire fence of a POW camp complete with his suit and war medals.

Bernard died in December 2014 aged ninety. The managing director of the home where he lived, Amanda Scott said of him: "Bernie caught the world's imagination when he made his 'surprise' trip to France and brought a huge amount of joy to a lot of people."

A short while later Bernard's widow also died and the couple left £600,000 in their wills to the Royal National Lifeboat Institution. In sharp contrast to the £600,000 stolen by Mr and Mrs Darwen back in 2002.

Talks Experience; At a talk in 2019 I was reminded by a gentleman of a story I would use at the end of police training sessions about managing missing person searches. It could be quite a tense lesson and this story offered light relief at the end of the day.

The double- glazing salesman telephoned the house. A small child answered in a very quiet voice.

"Hello" said the salesman, "Can I speak to your father?

"No," said the small voice, "He's busy"

"Ok, so can I speak to your mother please?" "No," said the small voice, "She's busy too"

The salesman could hear emergency sirens in the background. He asked the child, "Who else is in your house?"

"Well, there are policemen with dogs and firemen and social workers" answered the boy in an even quieter voice.

"Well, can I speak to one of them please?" "No, they're busy" said the child

"But what on earth are they all doing in your house?" asked the salesman, getting more worried by the minute.

The child replied with a quiet snigger, "THEY'RE ALL LOOKING FOR ME !!!

Chapter 7

Football matches and "the beautiful game"

Some people may remember the former home of Brighton and
Hove Albion football club. The Goldstone Ground (or just "The
Goldstone") was a football stadium and the home ground for the
team known locally as "The Seagulls" between 1902 and 1997. It is
now a retail park.

An interesting fact before we go any further: Between 1902 and
1997 when it closed, the ground had admitted 22.9 million
supporters to 2,174 games. The largest attendance had been an
astounding 36,747 when the Albion played Fulham on 27 December
1958. One of my regular duties as a constable during the late 1970s,
was to be bussed all the way over to Hove from Bognor Regis
whenever The Seagulls played a home match.

You may also remember that this was in the dying days of the "skin-
head" movement with their "Bovver boots": heavy Dr Martin
leather boots, braces and very short cropped hair. They also liked
nothing better than to get into fights at the merest excuse.

One of our regular duties was to stand at the turnstiles to assist the
stewards and search people entering the ground for offensive
weapons. These included sharpened coins which were a favourite
item for such people to launch at rival supporters. Sometimes a
police officer got in the way and ended up at the local hospital for
facial stitches.

Once at the turnstile these young skin heads were told they needed
to take their laces out of their Dr Martin boots (and lose them) as a
condition of entry to the football ground.

The theory of this tactic was that without laces they would be incapable of kicking anyone. If they tried to do so their prized boots would go flying.

Some boots had steel toe caps which could be very dangerous. Equally, some boots didn't. I thought it might be difficult to tell which were which, so I asked my sergeant at my first briefing how I could tell the difference. "Well PC Sadler, if you would like to step forward I will demonstrate how to check for the benefit of everyone else".

With a completely straight face, the burly sergeant came towards me and stood on my left foot. Not surprisingly, I yelped with pain. "There you go, son" he carried on "You are _not_ wearing steel toe capped boots, are you?"

So essentially, if I stood on a foot and they yelped then the skin head had to remove his boot laces which would prevent him kicking people. However, if they didn't yelp, then they had to get rid of their steel toe capped boots altogether and go into the match in their stockinged feet.

Just a quick question: Have you ever seen the film Zulu with Michael Cain? It was about the famous battle at Rorks Drift in January 1879 where 139 British soldiers successfully defended their garrison against an intense assault by up to four thousand Zulu warriors.

Well, in 1983 I was a patrol sergeant based in Crawley and, unfortunately, still being called to the Goldstone ground for football matches. On this particular Saturday, one of the London teams was playing (I think it was Milwall, but anyway it was something of a local derby game)

At the end of the match it was usual to let the away supporters out first and then "escort" them to Hove railway station to avoid any clashes in the street with home supporters. On this occasion, for some unknown reason, all the fans were going to be let out at the same time. I had a small team of about ten officers and we were standing in Old Shoreham Road at the end of the match.

I suddenly realised that a large group of the home fans were waiting at the top of the road near some traffic lights. They were quite clearly set to charge down the hill and attack the away fans who were starting to be let out of the gates behind us.

I told my officers to spread out across the closed off main road, take out their fourteen inches of wood (also known as a truncheon) and we would attempt to stop the ever-increasing horde from charging down the hill and causing mayhem.

My mind went back all those years to the film Zulu and the sequence where the Zulu warriors are massing on the hill before the charge down to Rorkes Drift! We stood there, facing the large group who were, by now, starting to run down the hill towards us. All of a sudden the group froze. They hesitated, then started to run in the opposite direction. I was amazed and to put it mildly quite relieved.

One of my young PCs turned to me and said, "I suppose you think that had something to do with us, don't you Sarge?" I said that I did and he replied, "Well think again and look behind us"

As I turned, I saw a line of snarling Alsatian police dogs straining on their leashes and coming up towards our thin blue line. My bubble had been well and truly burst. The fans sudden retreat had nothing to do with me or my team, but was all about self-preservation and the fear of getting a very nasty dog bite. Now, if only they had been at Rorkes Drift that day.

Just before we move on from police dogs, I want to mention how useful I found them. I had a habit of always checking to see how many dog handlers were on duty when I started my shift.

I valued their expertise immensely, especially on hot summer evenings when the night clubs turned out at 2am.

One day I was reading a news report about a particular case in another police force area where the Crown Prosecution Service (CPS) had insisted on being provided with a statement from a PC Peach. This followed a violent altercation with a criminal.

Despite the CPS being informed that PC Peach was in fact *a police dog*, they persisted with their demand. A joker in the relevant department apparently sent them a statement which read as follows:

Statement of: PC Peach;   *Age if under 18*: 4 years

Occupation: PD 4341   *Signature*: X

Body of witness statement: I chase him. I bite him. Bad man. He tasty. Good boy. Good boy Peach

The statement ended with a large black paw print.

Chapter 8

Political conferences and The Grand Hotel bombing

Certain dates stick in peoples' minds: Like being able to remember what you were doing:

- when the first man landed on the moon on July 20th 1969
- when you heard about the death of Princess Diana on August 31st 1997
- when the Twin Towers in New York were attacked on September 11th 2001

But how about 2:54 a.m on Friday 12th October 1984?

Like me, you were probably fast asleep in bed. That was the moment a bomb exploded on the sixth floor of the Grand Hotel, on Brighton seafront. The device had been planted by Provisional (IRA) operative Patrick Magee. It was intended to assassinate Prime Minister Margaret Thatcher and her cabinet, who were staying in the hotel for the Conservative Party conference all that week. Essentially, he was planning to do what Guy Fawkes had failed to do on 5th November 1605.

The bomb actually detonated at 2:54 a.m. Mrs Thatcher was still awake at that time, working on her speech in the Napoleon Suite. The blast badly damaged her bathroom but left her sitting room and bedroom unscathed. The PM and her husband, Denis, escaped injury. She calmly changed her clothes and was escorted to Brighton police station and then on to Sussex Police Headquarters at Lewes, where they stayed for the rest of the night.

2.54am Friday October 12th 1984

The Marks & Spencer store in Brighton's Western Road famously opened very early so those who had lost their clothes in the bombing could get new ones. Mrs Thatcher was determined the final day of the conference would go ahead as planned. The hunt for the bomber began immediately

IRA operative Patrick Magee had stayed in the Grand hotel under the false name of Roy Walsh during the weekend of 14–17 September 1984. During his stay, he planted the 20lb bomb (fitted with a long-delay timer) behind the bath panel in his room, number 629. A full 24 days later it exploded. I would often say to groups how weird it would be if you had stayed in room 629 during that intervening period. You could have lain in the bath, brushed your teeth at the sink and all the while the silent, long delay timer was progressively counting down to the final seconds.

And quite a few people had actually done just that, all of whom were traced, interviewed and eliminated; with one exception. Roy Walsh. After the explosion the IRA issued their now infamous statement:

> "Mrs. Thatcher will now realise that Britain cannot occupy our country and torture our prisoners and shoot our people in their own streets and get away with it. Today we were unlucky, but remember we only have to be lucky once. You will have to be lucky always. Give Ireland peace and there will be no more war."

Although the Prime Minister narrowly escaped the blast, five people connected with the Conservative Party were killed, including a sitting Conservative MP, Sir Anthony Berry (the party's Deputy Chief Whip). In addition, a further thirty one people were injured, some critically.

Sussex police traced and eliminated eight hundred people from fifty countries who had stayed at the hotel in the month before the attack. Anecdotally, there had been many "Mr Smiths" who had stayed at the hotel, with "Mrs Smith" of course. When detectives turned up at their true addresses shown on the registration cards there were many red-faced husbands who had to explain to their wives where they had been on the night in question. And, more to the point, who their companion was at the time, as it certainly wasn't them! For the sake of balance, there were a number of worried wives who had registered there under assumed names also.

Only one guest, who registered in the name of "Roy Walsh", could not be accounted for and he had actually stayed in room 629 where the explosion had occurred. This guest's true identity was finally revealed when a palm print on his hotel registration card matched a print taken from Patrick Magee some years earlier when he was first arrested as a juvenile in Norwich, where he grew up.

At the time detectives didn't want to issue a public alert, so they waited, hoping Magee would eventually reappear on the mainland. Police officers trailing another IRA suspect, Peter Sherry, arrested Magee in June 1985 at an IRA safe house in Glasgow, as he planned attacks on other British resorts.

In September 1986 at London's Central Criminal court, Patrick Joseph Magee, then aged thirty- five, was found guilty of planting the bomb, detonating it, and of five counts of murder. He received eight life sentences.

However, in 1999 Magee was released from prison, having served fourteen years, under the terms of the Good Friday Agreement. Whilst in prison he had completed a PhD course examining the representation of Irish Republicanism in 'Troubles' fiction. He left prison as *Dr* Patrick Magee.

Some days after the explosion I had been in charge of a team of officers tasked with securing the outer perimeter of this huge crime scene. Sadly, one of my team was missing. He had in fact been working on the night of the bombing and had been standing at the front of The Grand Hotel at the exact moment Magee's bomb exploded. Although injured and dazed from the effects of the falling masonry, he made a good recovery and returned to week some weeks later.

When I saw him walking down the corridor at Worthing police station, I went out to greet him. As he approached me I touched the arm of his tunic. *"Get off, Guv"* he said *"What are you doing?"* I said *"I am touching you for luck Dick, as you must be one of the luckiest people I will ever meet"* He had survived a massive bomb explosion and the tons of falling masonry had miraculously landed all around him with only smaller pieces actually hitting him.

In an interview for Irish republican publication An Phoblacht in August 2000 Patrick Magee said the following about that incident;

``I regret the deaths at Brighton,'' said Magee. *"I deeply regret that anybody had to lose their lives, but at the time did the Tory ruling class expect to remain immune from what their frontline troops were doing to us"* <u>Republican News</u> · <u>Thursday 31 August 2000</u>

From October 1984 onwards the nature of UK political conference policing changed forever. Whether it is held in Brighton, Blackpool, Bournemouth, Manchester or Birmingham, there are now extensive security plans in operation including;

- The creation of *an Island Site:* this area is extensively searched and sealed days before the conference starts.

- There are searches of surrounding areas. Even man -hole covers are lifted, checked and sealed with visible tape to prevent tampering.

- There is assistance on a huge scale from other police forces (called Mutual Aid)

- Air exclusion orders and even maritime exclusion orders where appropriate are established to keep the area secure.

- Long twelve hour shifts are worked by officers, with mass catering, briefing and rest sites set up.

Just by way of a local example, Operation Otter was the 2009 Labour Party conference held in Brighton. It was primarily a counter terrorism operation and, once again, the planning was based on the principle of the 'Island Site', a specially created secure area which incorporated the Brighton Centre, The De Vere Grand Hotel and the Hilton Metropole Hotel.

A quote in the local paper in the lead up to this conference said: *"Approximately 1000 police officers and support staff will be involved in the operation on a daily basis, either directly or indirectly, and it is acknowledged that an operation of this scale and complexity will inevitably pose a considerable burden on the force."*..........which is something of an understatement

The article also gave a positive slant: *"The event is seen as a major boost for businesses, injecting some £10m into the city's economy and is singularly the largest policing operation undertaken by Sussex Police.*

Talk experience One group I visited in Brighton was called The Sparks who turned out to be retired Marks and Spencer workers. One photograph I show at talks is of a lady "dressing" Sir Keith Joseph (one of Mrs Thatcher's minister caught up in the hotel bombing) in the Western Road store. He is shown in his dressing gown being provided with new suit, shirt and shoes by the shop assistant. It turned out that some of the ladies in this group had been bussed in especially early to help with this task.

I asked one lady what she remembered of that unique early morning shift. "Well dear" she said, "It was just like walking onto a film set with lots of people I had only ever seen on the TV, but they were all covered in dust and wearing pyjamas"

Two other unusual incidents came about as a direct result of my limited involvement in that operation in October 1984. Firstly, I was giving my talk "A policeman's lot can be quite an interesting one" to a retired professional group, when a member told me that the Brighton bomber, Pat Magee, now worked for a peace and reconciliation charity. This seemed to be rather ironic given the image I still had of the gaping hole at the front of The Grand Hotel. I set about to find out more.

My "informant" turned out to be correct. Pat Magee was in fact linked to an organisation called Building Bridges for Peace. Their strap line was "A non- profit organisation promoting peace and conflict resolution throughout the world".

I located the relevant website and discovered that it was founded in 2009 by a Jo Berry to promote peace and conflict transformation around the world. That name rang a bell with me from the terrible events of 1984.

As I read on I learned that Jo had actually founded the charity after losing her father, Sir Anthony Berry, in the Brighton Grand Hotel bombing. He had been the sitting MP murdered that terrible night. Since 2000 she had been working with Magee, the man responsible for the death of her father.

The organisation's website quoted Jo as saying:

"On October 12th 1984 my father, Sir Anthony Berry and four others were killed in the bombing of the Grand Hotel, Brighton as they attended the Conservative Party Conference. I made a personal decision just two days later, to bring something positive out of this emotionally shattering trauma and to try and understand those who had killed him".

Jo arranged to meet the man who had planted the bomb and in 2000 she sat down with Magee at a friends house in Dublin. Her intention was to hear his story so that she could experience him as a human being. Understandably, she was scared but felt she needed to see him and speak to him.

On her website she goes on to explain; "At first he began to express his political perspective, which, though I was familiar with, was hard to hear. But I could see he was a sensitive and intelligent person."

And later, Jo concludes "Then something changed. He stopped talking and said he didn't know who he was any more, he wanted to hear my anger, my pain and what could he do to help. It was as if he had taken off his political hat and had now opened up and became vulnerable. The conversation was very different after that and a new journey started."

Suffice to say that a new working relationship was formed. They have now travelled extensively to extoll the value of peace and conflict transformation. I found out there was to be an event in Islington in February 2013 at which the couple were to be the key speakers.

I paid my £10 and set off for this event. As I was travelling up the escalator at Angel underground station, I noticed a shortish man with a walking stick standing a few feet ahead of me. It was Patrick Magee en route to the function. The hairs on the back of my neck stood up as my mind rushed back to Brighton seafront in October 1984. At the event a short while later Jo and Pat Magee sat on stools with a table containing a red rose between them. They talked about the work of the charity and where they had visited on their "journey" during their time together.

It appeared to me the organisers were less than keen for questions from the audience at the end. However, I had travelled some distance and was not going to be denied the chance to ask Magee a question. I stood and asked; "Knowing what you know now after your twelve year "journey" with Jo, do you believe that violence can ever be justified in a political struggle?"

He replied that the "Troubles" came about from a position of weakness on behalf of the minority catholic population in Northern Ireland. There was a feeling they had no alternative but to defend the minority population from attack by the Loyalist majority community.

He went on to say; "I regret all the deaths and injuries caused by myself and my comrades. No one would want what they did on their conscience unless they felt they had no option".

For me, the most telling section was when he began to talk about the Grand Hotel bombing. He continued: "It was just another operation. It was part of our campaign which targeted the "architects of repression" on the mainland and we felt it would force the government of the day to deal with the issue"

Just before the meeting ended Jo Berry had one final, rather poignant comment to make. She said her daughter had asked her to ask Magee the following question; "Did he not think about Grandad when he planted that bomb in the hotel?" Jo said she had tried to explain that he wasn't visualising people when the bomb was planted. She also said that if she been through the experiences that he had gone through she wondered if she might have made similar choices.

The second unusual occurrence happened in 2014 when I received an unexpected telephone call.

A woman called me out of the blue and said that her aunt had been at one of my Women's Institute police talks. She had mentioned that one of my subjects was the Grand Hotel bombing and she thought her niece might be interested in talking to me. It transpired that the woman on the end of the telephone was called Julie Everton and she was in the process of co-writing a play about that very incident.

She then rather surprised me by asking if I would be prepared to meet her and her colleague, Josie Melia. Once I had satisfied myself these ladies were who they said they were, I agreed. Julie was at the time a senior lecturer in Drama and Scriptwriting at the University of Brighton.

Having sat down at Café Rouge in Haywards Heath, Julie suddenly produced a tape recorder and asked if I minded if they recorded our conversation. I quipped that, in my former life it would have been me starting the tape recorder, but I readily agreed to her request.

I wanted to know what research they had done already before meeting me. "Well" said Julie, "We went over to interview Pat in Belfast". This really did surprise me and I asked "Who do you mean, Patrick Magee?" "Oh yes" she replied. I was intrigued to know where they had met him.

"At the Europa Hotel in Belfast" she said. I began laughing and she asked me what was so funny. I replied "You do know that the Europa Hotel is known as the "most bombed hotel in Europe" and in fact the "most bombed hotel in the world". It had suffered thirty six bomb attacks during the Troubles. I thought how ironic it had been

79

for these two women to meet a convicted IRA bomber in that particular hotel. Although I had only played a marginal policing role after the explosion, I had retained many press cuttings and reports which I was happy to lend them. None of this material was secret and had been in the public domain at the time.

Sometime later I received an invitation from Julie to attend The Cockpit Theatre in **Marylebone, which** is notable as London's first purpose-built theatre in the round built since the Great Fire of London. The play which Julie and Josie had created was about to have its first script run through on stage. I took my daughter, Rachael along as she worked in London at the time.

The play, entitled *"The Bombing of the Grand hotel"* was described in the publicity sheet as: "A visceral new history play tells the story of the unlikely relationship between Pat Magee, who planted the bomb, and Jo Berry, whose father was killed in the blast….it is a thought provoking and moving exploration of the political pressures and personal triggers surrounding a key moment of extreme public violence within a continuing struggle for change".

Imagine my surprise when the reading reached scene 15:

Scene; *Outside the main door of the Grand Hotel.*

The original script then went as follows;

Pc Sadler: (banging his personal police radio) Bloody batteries….always running out

Philip (a conference delegate) All quiet on the Western front?

Pc Sadler Off to the agent's ball, sir?

Philip Just waiting for my wife. Must say, you're doing a jolly good job here. Security's been very low key. Unobtrusive.

Pc Sadler. Glad you think so.

Amazingly, Julie and Josie had named a character in their play after *me*.

However, on a later occasion when I took my wife to see the finished production at the Brighton Festival in summer 2015, that particular scene (*and Pc Sadler himself*) had been consigned to the cutting room floor!

Talks experience The conservative party's Agents Ball was always held on the final night of conference week (Thursday 11th October 1984). At one of my talks an elderly gentleman told me he had actually danced with Mrs Thatcher at around 1030pm that night; in other words a mere four and a half hours before the explosion. He said that she was a good dancer and "quite charming".

As he lived within easy travelling distance of Brighton, he didn't actually stay in the Grand Hotel that night and only found out about the bombing the following day.

At a different talk in Brighton, I showed a number of photographs of the decimated Grand Hotel and of Mrs Thatcher. A gentleman on the second row was obviously eager to say something but decided against it. As I had anticipated, the gentleman waited for all his friends to leave and approached me as I was packing away my equipment.

He said that he thought Mrs Thatcher had been a very polarising Prime Minister, to which I agreed. He went on to tell me his strong views on the way she had mishandled the Miners Strike in the mid 1980s. He then finished off by telling me the following, and I could then see why he had been reluctant to voice his opinion earlier.

"You know, when I woke up that morning and realised <u>she</u> had survived that bomb I knew there was no God. I know, I shouldn't say that, but that is how I felt!"

A question which is often asked of me when talking about the Grand Hotel bombing is; "What happened to the occupants of Room 629 that night?"

Sir Donald Maclean and his wife Muriel had attended the conference that week as he was president of the Scottish Conservatives. Maclean, an Ayrshire optometrist, was asleep in room 629 when the bomb detonated behind the bath panel in their en-suite bathroom.

The huge blast ripped out the front wall of his bedroom and Maclean awoke to find himself in a sitting position a floor below his room, trapped by a mass of rubble and debris. As he looked around, totally dazed, there was no sign of Muriel.

A surgeon and two firemen were lowered on ropes into the void to give Maclean assistance. Working by torchlight and still suspended on ropes, it took the three of them two and a half hours to free Maclean.

His wife, when found, had ostensibly sustained only facial injuries and a badly broken leg. However, her injuries turned out to far more severe and after a five week fight to save her life, doctors lost their battle. Sir Donald survived and later went on to remarry. He died in 2010.

Another question which fascinates people is what happened to whoever was asleep in the bedrooms on the seventh floor above room 629. Harvey Thomas was one of those people and is one of the most fascinating characters caught up in this affair. **Thomas, the organiser of the Conservative Party conference, had** spent fourteen years as press adviser and conference organiser for Margaret Thatcher and the Conservative party. His bedroom was actually on the seventh floor, just above the seat of the explosion. He was thrown through the roof of the hotel by the night-time blast and then left buried in rubble, dangling above a five-storey drop.

Speaking to the Times newspaper from his hospital bed the following day, he said: "I was sound asleep and I felt a tremendous noise and crashing. I thought it was an earthquake. Then I realized that you do not have earthquakes in Brighton, at least not during a Tory party conference." He also recalled how from his trapped position he had needed to scratch and claw to keep the rubble away from his face. "I needed to squirm to stay away from the water cascading from a fractured pipe. At least I hope it was water!"

Thomas hung in his wedged position for two and a half hours until being rescued. Finally, they dug him out without even a broken bone. What kept him going was the thought of his pregnant wife and unborn child.

Harvey was a particularly well- built man and he recalls saying to the Brighton firemen who rescued him that he wanted to walk down to the ground floor. The fire crew insisted he had to be carried on a stretcher due to what he had gone through.

When they reached the front of the hotel the Chief fire officer apparently said to him; "If we'd known how heavy you were we'd have let you walk down!"

The Grand Hotel was reopened in 1986 at a triumphant ceremony attended by Margaret Thatcher. At this time Thomas confided that some weeks after the bombing he had received a bill from the Grand for his room on that final night. He said, 'I wrote back to the hotel and said: "Would you mind giving me half a night's discount, because the room didn't exist after 3am?"

My wife had always known about my fascination for the Grand Hotel. For my sixtieth birthday she secretly planned an overnight stay in the hotel. On arrival we were shown to the second floor and into a room with a fantastic sea view and a balcony, a couple of chairs and a small table. I saw that the gold lettered sign for the "Grand" was actually attached to our balcony which made it easy to identify from the seafront.

My wife had also mentioned to the hotel receptionist my "morbid fascination" for Patrick Magee and the events of 12th October 1984. She asked if it would be possible for me to look inside room 629 (obviously if there was no guest in residence)

Luckily the room was vacant and the young lady pressed the lift button for the sixth floor. She then told us that the bedrooms had been renumbered but she assured me the room we were about to enter had actually been 629 in 1984. The view was stunning. It was so high up and overlooked the ruined West Pier. I glanced into the bathroom and imagined Magee prising off the bath panel and very carefully inserting the bomb, complete with its long delay timer.

The view from what had been Room 629 of The Grand Hotel

A few days later I checked my records and discovered my wife and I had been sleeping in the actual room occupied by Norman and Margaret Tebbit the night the bomb exploded.

Mrs Tebbitt, who was confined to a wheel chair after the terrible injuries she sustained that dreadful night, passed away in December 2020.

Whilst remaining entirely a-political at all my police talks, I can't help but mention an incident that happened to the then Prime Minister, Tony Blair. Back in 200,7 shortly before he decided to hand over the reins of the country to Gordon Brown, Mr Blair visited Brighton.

He was there to launch the next stage of his governments' Respect strategy. He also wanted to say thank you to all the police officers who had made sure the Grand Hotel hadn't gone bang on his watch. This was despite the fact he always stayed at The Metropole Hotel during Conference season.

Mr Blair looked rather surprised when, shaking hands with a young PC Holly Hallahan, she curtsied in front of him. "Oh, you don't have to do that for me you know" said the PM with one of his famously dazzling smiles. "Oh yes I do" replied Holly, "It's just won me a five quid bet".

Oh, what I would have given to have been in the room when that happened.

Chapter 9

The things people have said at talks.

It's one thing setting yourself up as a "speaker" and managing to pass the "Speakers selection" meetings for the Women's Institute. It's another thing actually getting bookings to attend meetings. And then it's a third thing to turn up on the appointed date and be expected!

I say this rather tongue in cheek as, on five occasions so far, I have been "double booked" by groups. The first time was particularly galling, as I had driven around forty miles from my home in West Sussex into the wilds of affluent rural Surrey.

I arrived at the village hall with about half an hour to spare. I liked to give myself plenty of time to carry my suitcase, screen, PA system etc into the hall to set everything up before the meeting started.

As I walking from the car park, dragging my suitcase behind me and carrying my old policeman's helmet under my arm, a lady came out of the hall and appeared to be waiting for me. "Hello dear" she said, "Where are the other seventeen of you?"

I looked at her and said "Seventeen? There's just me". "Oh, so you're not part of the male voice choir we've booked today" she replied. It turned out their rather forgetful speaker's secretary had booked myself and also the local choir. We decided that it would probably be best if I just left quickly and drive the forty miles all the way home.

I was given a small sum to cover my fuel costs and drove immediately to the nearby National Trust property at Polesden Lacey. This is an Edwardian house and estate, located on the North

Downs near Dorking. I enjoyed a stroll around the house and gardens, finishing off with a most agreeable cream tea. And yes, I did get a re-booking from the group and went back the following year. No choir turned up that day.

In the early days of providing talks it became apparent those who were due to introduce me often struggled with what to say.

To make things easier for them (and so I always knew what was coming) I decided that each talk would have a printed "blurb" which could be read out if needs be. By way of example:

The title of Neil's talk today is:

A POLICEMAN'S LOT CAN BE QUITE AN INTERESTING ONE !

Neil joined the Sussex Police in 1978, after two years teaching on the Isle of Man.

Starting as a constable in Bognor Regis, he progressed through the ranks on uniform patrol duties across Sussex.

Neil's final posting was in national and international police training working briefly in Hong Kong, Abu Dhabi and Trinidad, with the odd exotic spell in Horsham, Haywards Heath and Crawley.

He retired from the police in 2008, the same year his younger daughter joined and inherited his warrant number of *"DOUBLE O 6 " (006).....YES SERIOUSLY*

I deliberately typed these printed introductions in large font to assist those who might have sight difficulties. At one memorable talk in a chilly village hall the weather was particularly cold and icy. When I entered the venue it was freezing and I was told the heating had broken down and was I happy to continue. Bearing in mind all the ladies were sitting there in their coats, gloves and scarves and had made the effort to come out, I felt it would be churlish to decline.

As normal, I gave the president my laminated introduction card but when she stood up at the start of my talk she was shivering quite badly. As she read out the card she said; "Neil joined Sussex Police *in 1908"* completely misreading my start date. I smiled and looked out at forty ladies whose facial expression said it all. Gosh, he's worn well!

An even funnier incident happened as I was setting up my equipment at another Women's Institute meeting. The room was filling slowly and I was introduced to the president of the group, a lady I would guess to be about eighty five years of age. She continued to stand just behind me, scanning the arrivals for any new members.

As a younger woman approached her, I could hear the following conversation unfold. "Hello dear" said the President, "Are you a new member by any chance?" "Yes I am" replied the other lady, "I have just retired and have always wanted to join the WI but never had the time. I am so looking forward to it ."At this point the President obviously wondered what the woman had been doing before retirement and decided to ask her. "Well, for forty years I was a nuclear physicist" answered the potential new member.

I shall never forget what happened next. The President just looked at the woman and as calmly as possible called out in a loud voice "Who's doing teas today?", completely non plussed by the other woman's admission.

As a police Inspector there were certain tasks with which I had to get involved by statute. Reviewing the lawful detention of people in custody, administering police cautions as an alternative to summons or court appearance and arranging and running identification parades (or Line-ups) were just a few of these tasks.

One of the most memorable cautions I ever administered involved a young primary school girl. On this particular evening I was asked to go to Horsham police station where a member of Social Services had a juvenile ready to be cautioned for a drug dealing offence.

To say I was a little surprised when I entered the interview room is putting it mildly. There, sitting next to the social worker, was a girl of about ten or eleven years of age, still wearing her school uniform. It transpired she had been coerced by her parents to take a small quantity of herbal cannabis into her local primary school with the intention of selling it in the playground at break time. Any proceeds were to be passed back to the parents. She had hidden the drugs in one of those hollow plastic Kinder chocolate egg boxes.

Not surprisingly, she had been taken into care as soon as this offence was discovered by the teaching staff and I was expected to administer a caution and release her back into the care of the Social Services.

After I had said my piece, I asked her if there was anything she wanted to ask me or if there was anything she didn't understand. In the majority of cases, most youngsters just want to get out of the police station as quickly as possible

Now English is a fantastic language, but it can be very easy to misinterpret certain words. On this occasion the young girl looked at me and, with total innocence, asked me if she could have her *"pot"* back; by which I understood her to mean the Kinder egg container

Unfortunately, the social worker had, like me, lived through the 1970s and thought by "pot" she meant the cannabis which she had concealed inside the plastic egg.

She was infuriated at the cheek of the young girl and began haranguing her, only for me to stop her mid-flow and clarify that it was, in fact, only the little yellow egg container she wanted back.

I ripped open the plastic evidence bag and handed back the young girl's prized possession. She confided that she liked hiding her other small toys inside the plastic egg.

I must admit that was one occasion where I had a lump in my throat, as this young girl was about the same age as my elder daughter at the time. There but for the grace of God, etc.

Talks experience. I had presented my original Policeman's lot talk at a Women's Institute meeting in Pevensey, East Sussex. At the end it was time for a cup of tea and piece of cake and my wife, Julie, came in from the car park to join me.

A lady approached and asked me if I had been stationed at Bognor Regis in 1978. I said yes, but not until the end of the year. She then asked if I remembered working with a PC (name forgotten). I said I didn't recall that name and asked her why. She replied "I *was* married to him". The way she said this should have raised alarm bells.

I asked if he was still "in the job" to which she replied "Oh no dear. He was asked to leave after he got a bit violent with the public. Then he got violent with me, so I left him" My wife and I just looked at each other in amazement at this rather personal revelation. We thought the lady had left but she came back and said the immortal words, "Oh by the way,dear he's a she now you know. Good night" and she just walked off.

On another occasion a lady told me her father in law had been a constable in London during the blitz. Very innocently I said something like "Oh, that's nice" She replied "No its not. He wasn't nice. We all hated him!"

I was rather taken aback by this response and asked why she had hated him. She replied "Well, he would go around after a bombing raid and arrest all the looters who were taking things from people's damaged houses. He'd then go back and actually stole the things himself. That's why we hated him!".

A little game I played with myself involved putting codes against entries in my record book after every talk if food had been offered. "VGF" stood for "very good food" whilst "SB" had nothing to do with Special Branch but "stale biscuits". This was where the group had opened their large tin of biscuits in January and offered them to me in the September!

Still my most memorable experience was at the WI meeting in Sussex where there appeared to be a superb, full spread of sandwiches, cakes and buns at the rear of the hall. When I jokingly said to the President "Oh you shouldn't have gone to all this trouble for me you know."

She replied "We haven't, dear. This is what's left over from Mavis's funeral tea yesterday after we buried her. If It's not eaten today it all goes in the bin".

During my Policeman's Lot: talk I would often mention a notorious gangster called "Mad" Frankie Fraser and show a slide with his unmistakable face.

The reason I did this was that he had only recently become the oldest person in England ever to be served with an ASBO (an anti social behaviour order) after what the red top newspapers called "A bust up with a fellow resident at his care home". Even at 89 years of age he still couldn't behave himself.

But why the nickname "Mad"? It transpired Fraser had been certified insane on three separate occasions. The first was when he was in the army during the second world war, the next time when he was sent to Cane Hill psychiatric hospital in Coulsdon, Surrey, and the third when he was transferred from Durham prison to Broadmoor.

Fraser's 42 years served in over 20 different prisons in the UK were often punctuated by violence. He was involved in prison riots and frequently fought with prison officers and fellow inmates. He also attacked various prison governors.

In 1980 Fraser was 'excused boots' as he claimed he had problems with his feet because another prisoner had dropped a bucket of boiling water on them after Fraser had hit him.

Amazingly, he was permitted to wear slippers. In the Guardian obituary following his death in November 2014, it mentioned how Fraser decided on whether to work for the Kray "Firm" or throw his hat in with their bitter rivals, the Richardson gang.

"He was courted by both the Kray Twins and the Richardson gang. He chose the latter because they had taken sides on behalf of his sister's husband, Tommy Brindle, who had received a heavy beating by the Rosa brothers from the Elephant and Castle".

Fraser received 10 years for his part in the so-called Richardson Gang torture trial. It was said that he pulled out the teeth of his victims with a pair of pliers.

Throughout his life he denied the justice of this conviction, but was happy to trade off it. At signing sessions for his books he was always willing to be photographed pretending to extract a tooth with pliers brought along by the fans.

Talks experience After one talk a lady with a pronounced cockney accent told me a funny story relating to Fraser and teeth. She had once worked in a chemist shop in the East End of London and Frankie Fraser often popped in to purchase things. One day he was in her shop when a young woman approached the medicine counter holding her jaw. She asked this lady if she could suggest anything for raging toothache.

She immediately pointed towards Fraser, who was minding his own business, and suggested the young woman have a word with him, as he was well practiced at tooth extraction and would be bound to help her!

Fraser had four sons, three of whom followed in their father's footsteps, to one extent or another. His fourth son, Francis, in Fraser's joking words, "let me down" by having no criminal career at all.

The same lady told me that not many people know that gangsters Ronnie and Reggie Kray were actually the last people ever to be imprisoned in The Tower of London way back in 1952, for failing to report for national service.

Some of my bookings have been in extremely nice hotels, restaurants and even Masonic halls and synagogues. I often ate lunch and then was expected to stand up as the after-lunch "entertainment".

On some occasions the chairman or president would say a few words or introduce a new member, but only at Women's Institute meetings would we all sing the first two verses of Jerusalem.

At Probus lunches a new member would often be expected to give a potted history of their former working life. Whilst sometimes these proved stuttering or rather dry (or both) the following example was exceptional.

This was as told by a retired vicar at a Probus lunch in Littlehampton when introducing himself as a new member to the group. Everyone had expected a long winded, sermon-like speech. Instead he came out with this gem. He related it as if it was a true story about a new vicar, which made the punchline even more effective and comical. It went like this;

"A recently ordained vicar took his first service in his new parish. He'd worked hard on his sermon. It was so important to make a good first impression. Admittedly, it was rather long and laborious, but at the end he was pretty satisfied with his inaugural performance

At the end of the service he was very excited and eagerly awaited his new congregation outside the church door. A little girl and her father approached him and he began to shake the father's hand.

The little girl suddenly said, in a very loud voice, "When I grow up, I'm going to become a millionaire, make lots of money and give half to you, Vicar."

The minister was overwhelmed with her generosity and asked her why she would want to do that? The little girl replied, with the innocence of youth, "Because my Daddy says you are the poorest preacher he's ever heard!"   Boom, boom.

At many Womens' Institute meetings they still practice singing Jerusalem. A strange thing happened one winter at one such meeting in Kent. As I walked into the hall I noticed there were no spare chairs for me to sit on whilst the meeting went ahead. I glanced around the room and saw a large pile of chairs right in front of the piano. Without thinking, I walked over and removed the top chair, taking it to the other side of the room. All of a sudden, a very short, wizened woman entered the room and made straight for the piano, sheaf of music in hand. She pulled the pile of chairs back carefully but suddenly realised there were insufficient chairs to let her reach the keyboard comfortably! Jerusalem was played at a very slow pace that afternoon.

To finish my second Policeman's Lot talk, I would show a slide of a T-shirt worn by a Hells Angel motor cyclist. It had a series of statements on the back. These talks coincided with the never-ending, protracted arguments about the UK leaving the European Union (between 2016-2020).The reason I loved showing groups this shirt was that it made apparent fun of so many national stereotypes. Te slogan read as follows:

> "Heaven is where the police are British, the chefs Italian, the mechanics German, the lovers French and it's all organised by the Swiss.
>
> Hell is where the police are German, the chefs British, the mechanics French, the lovers Swiss and it's all organised by the Italians"

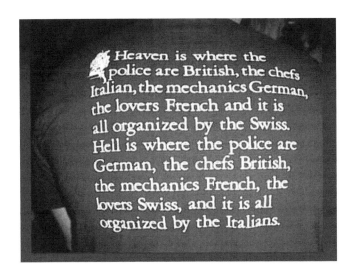

As seen on the back of a Hells Angel motorcyclist

On one occasion I was giving this talk at a regional meeting of the Womens' British Legion and was really looking forward to a sumptuous afternoon tea. My wife had turned up to collect me before the tea was served. As she approached me, I was just about to tell how well the talk had gone but she said "I think we need to leave as soon as possible".

Having seen the plates of cakes and sandwiches I was in no hurry, but she insisted. I asked her why it was important to leave so fast and she said "Well that lady over there doesn't seem too impressed with you after you showed the slide of the T- shirt".

Too late, as the woman she had pointed out was making her way quite purposefully towards me. She was very elegant, well dressed and as she spoke she had a pronounced foreign accent.

"Excuse me, young man" she said "I need to take issue with you as I am Swiss". My mind went blank, as I couldn't recall what the shirt said about the Swiss.

She then said, "My husband can't be too bad a lover as we actually have six children you know!" Cue an early departure with no nice scones and cakes that afternoon!

I had only just started giving talks back in 2011 but one of the first places I went to was Bexhill on Sea. It was a very hot summers morning and the organiser couldn't work out how to open the windows to let in some fresh air.

The group was almost exclusively female with just two men, one of whom was the organiser. He approached me and asked how long I normally talked for. I said "Forty five minutes" and he said "Make it thirty".

I explained that I normally asked members of the group to choose which subjects I should talk about. He was adamant that I should choose say, three subjects at the most and just tell them!

He then said "Do you want me to pay you now?" I replied "But you haven't heard me yet" But he said not to worry and gave me cash upfront! He ended with a friendly warning. "Don't worry if some of them just get up and walk out while you're talking. Some of them have a very short attention span and some need to catch a bus home!"

It is always disappointing when a story you have been telling audiences for years turns out to be either "fake news" (don't get me started on President Trump!) or is no longer occurring.

For a number of years I would show a slide which asked, "In which European country should you not try and out run the police?" Many people would suggest Germany (think Porsche, BMW or Audi) and then someone would pipe up with Italy.

I would then show a fantastic slide of a pale blue police car being used in Italy. It was no run- of- the mill Fiat or Alfa Romeo. It was, in fact, a Lamborghini Gallardo, complete with police number plates and flashing blue lights.

An Italian motor magazine said of it at the time: "It won't be a mere panda car, with high-speed motorway use its specialty. As well as chasing down criminals it comes complete with a defibrillator and the ability to transport emergency blood transfusions, making it a potential lifesaver, too." (Evo October 2008)

The car was surrounded by half a dozen **Carabinieri**, all eager to get behind the wheel.
It had a top speed of 202mph, could reach 100mph in just under 4 seconds, but only managed 11 mpg: do the cops care? Of course not, they are going to have some real fun at the office and not be paying for the fuel.

I used to tell groups that this particular super car had previously belonged to one of the Mafia bosses from Naples. After a police raid, they had arrested him, seized his yachts in the harbour, all his supercars and all the cash stashed under the mattress. Then someone with a sense of humour had the fastest of the cars resprayed blue and given to the traffic cops, no doubt to rub salt into the wounds.

It was only recently, when searching the internet that I found the following headline which rather burst my bubble on this anecdote.

"Italian police to stop driving Mafia Ferraris and Porsches": Crime fighting in Italy is set to become less glamorous for police after the government announced it was scrapping the use of luxury cars seized from Mafia Godfathers because of high running costs. They will no longer be allowed to get behind the wheels of Ferrari, Lamborghini, Maserati or Porsche cars that had been confiscated from crime chiefs and will return to their standard issue Fiat and Alfa Romeo. In a U turn, the government has announced they can no longer afford to allow police forces to use the luxury cars because running costs and spare parts are too expensive.

Talks experience At a talk in Hove I was just packing away my equipment when a short, well tanned gentleman approached me. He said, "I think you are wrong about the Lamborghini police car having been seized from a Mafia chief in Naples. The Mafia are not in that area; it is the Camorra who originated in that area and dominate Naples. There is the Mafia in Sicily and the 'Ndrangheta who are the organized crime syndicate based in Calabria in the extreme south of Italy." Something in the way he said this told me he knew an awful lot about this subject. I thanked the Italian gentlemen and left the meeting fairly swiftly. After that I didn't mention the Mafia by name in the story ever again.

A section of my second police talk discusses famous police cars in film and TV. I enjoyed showing the maroon Triumph Roadster driven by John Nettles as DS Bergerac on Jersey in the police programme of the same name. The next picture showed DI Morse (John Thaw) leaning against his Jaguar.

And then I showed the Mark 2 Ford Granada 2.8iS as used in the final season of "The Sweeney". These cars came courtesy of Ford, whose sense for product placement was second to none in the British motor industry.

The first episode of "The Sweeney" was transmitted in January 1975 and after that, British television would never be quite the same again. The Ford Granada would be forever associated with flared trousers, lots of shouting of "Guv'nor" and car chases through London which the "baddies" would never win.

When Euston Films, the film division of Thames Television, commenced work on the pilot "Regan", the Ford motor company at Dagenham already had a long-established tradition of product placement in major television and film productions. They offered the makers of the series free use of the Granadas but on condition only the good guys drove them.

A more recent example of excessive use of one car brand was rumoured to occur in the film "Fifty shades of Grey". This was the 2015 American erotic romantic drama film based on E. L. James' 2011 novel of the same name. I had read somewhere that the Audi car company had been mentioned almost exclusively throughout the book.

Purely on the grounds of research you understand, I decided to visit Cineworld at Crawley and check this out for myself. I went on a day when my wife was volunteering at a local National Trust gardens, as I knew she would be less interested in "car spotting" than I was.

To save myself any embarrassment, I carefully checked the starting time of the film so that I could walk in when all the main lights had been dimmed. I duly bought my ticket and pushed open the cinema doors hoping not to bump into my next door neighbour, or even worse my local vicar!

Unbelievably, as I approached the front of the auditorium, all the house lights suddenly came on. I was left standing there looking up at about one hundred cinema goes: all female and not one man in sight except for yours truly.

There was nothing for it but to trudge rather sheepishly up to the back row to take my seat. But back to my reason for being there with the hundred women from Crawley. The main character, Christian Grey, drives an Audi R8 Spyder. As the story progresses he buys Anastasia and his other girlfriends Audi A3 cars.

He says it is because he believes they are (to quote the text of the book) "the safest car on the market".

I subsequently located a dog- eared copy of the first Fifty Shades book and laboriously scanned its pages for Audi references. I found sixteen entries in total. What I do for creative accuracy!

Whilst many of the things people have said to me have had a comical side to them, there have been a number of times when they were either terribly poignant or incredibly tragic or both. Three incidents have stayed with me in particular.

At a morning talk in Haywards Heath, a lady came up to me while I was setting up my screen and projector. "Excuse me" she said, "But are you going to be talking about local crimes today?" I said that most of my case studies were more of a national nature. She then said something which made my blood run cold. In a quiet voice she said, "I was just worried you might have been talking about my eleven year old son who was murdered in the woods nearby back in the 1980s". She then went on to tell me, in quite graphic detail, about the tragedy which had occurred not a mile from where we were standing that day.

It transpired that her son had been playing in the woods when a young man had killed him. Whilst in Lewes prison, the accused had committed suicide. All the way through that talk I was conscious of the bereaved mother sitting on the second row in front of me and of the desperately sad story she had told me.

A similar event happened some years later at a talk in south London. An elderly lady approached me at the end of the talk and asked if she could seek my opinion on something. I wrongly assumed it would be something like whether she should pay a parking fine or take a speed awareness course after being caught speeding. It couldn't have been more different.

She said "Do you think I should write to the Home Secretary, as I fear my son's murderer is due to be released and they promised they would advise me when it was going to happen?" Quite clearly this was something I was poorly equipped to advise on, especially as I knew nothing about this poor lady's situation.

She went on to explain that in November 1994, her son, John had been a trainee manager for Woolworths. He was just twenty one years of age when he was stabbed through the heart with a kitchen knife at the Woolworths store in Teddington, south west London. He had attempted to stop a man seizing cash from a till.

At the Old Bailey trial, the murderer, unemployed Ian Kay, 28, had regarded his victim as "fair game and a necessary hazard in a robbery". The prosecuting barrister had said: "He (Kay) had no regrets for what he had done." The prosecutor continued, "He said in chilling terms that if someone was stupid enough to have a go and try to stop him then they got what they deserved,"

Dubbed "The Woolworth Killer", Kay was found guilty and sentenced to be detained in a secure mental hospital indefinitely. The recommended minimum term would have kept him behind bars until 2017, until he was fifty years of age. It was 2017 when I was having this conversation with the bereaved mother.

The lady also told me that while Kay was in Broadmoor psychiatric hospital, he had tried to murder Peter Sutcliffe, the notorious "Yorkshire Ripper". I said to the lady that, although the target release date might have been 2017, I would be very surprised if it went ahead, especially if Kay had gone on to commit yet another heinous crime whist detained.

When I got home, I looked into both of these incidents and discovered that, according to a Broadmoor source, a row had developed between Kay and Sutcliffe at the special hospital. Before staff could reach him, Kay had attacked Sutcliffe, stabbing at his face with a felt tip pen. It was thought Sutcliffe was in danger of losing his sight after being stabbed in both eyes with the implement.

On another occasion in 2019 I was at an evening booking in Kent near West Kingsdown. This was of particular interest to me as the village hall was located about five hundred yards from a property of tragic notoriety in police circles.

A bold headline in the Sun newspaper had caught my attention only a few months before.

It read: "M25 killer Kenneth Noye's old home where he killed a cop and let lions prowl the grounds up for sale at £2.8 million".

It transpired that notorious career criminal Kenneth Noye, once dubbed Britain's most dangerous man, built the mock Tudor house and called it Hollywood Cottage with the proceeds from a lucrative smuggling empire.

The estate was flanked by high walls and protected by an elaborate network of CCTV cameras when Noye owned it. High-strength security lights could light up the garden at a moment's notice.

In January 1985 a pair of undercover police officers crept into the vast garden to investigate the £26 million Brinks Matt bullion robbery, but were soon surrounded by Noye's three snarling rottweilers.

One of the officers escaped over the wall. However, the other, DC John Fordham, was savagely attacked by the knife-wielding gang boss. He was stabbed in the heart with such force that the blade severed a rib clean in two. The detective died on the way to hospital with six separate knife wounds. Noye was found not guilty of murder after persuading a jury that he acted in self-defence. He blew kisses at jurors as he was allowed to walk free.

But less than a year later he was back in the dock after melting down some of the stolen Brinks Matt gold bullion. Amazingly, eleven gold bars were found hidden in his vast Kent mansion. After eight years in jail, Noye was released and back to his old tricks

It is believed Noye sold the house for an estimated £1m shortly before murdering electrician Stephen Cameron in 1996 during a furious "road rage" incident on an M25 sliproad near Swanley in Kent. Noye then adsconded to Spain but, thankfully, the law finally caught up with him and he was jailed for life. The gangster, 72, was released from a life sentence in June 2019.

He reportedly made the decision to sell his Kent house whilst in prison after local police officers annoyed his wife by erecting a permanent (and frequently vandalised) memorial to DC Fordham at the end of their drive.

On the evening of my talk, I managed to locate both the house and DC Fordham's memorial stone. It was after the talk had finished that I casually mentioned Kenneth Noye to a member of the audience.

Also, that I had heard he had been released from prison only recently. The lady gave me a curious look and said that soon after moving to the village she and her husband had realised it was best not to mention Noye by name.

I asked why and she said that they never knew to whom they were speaking, as some still viewed him as a bit of a Robin Hood figure. She ended with an interesting aside. She told me that Noye's sister still lived locally and was a pillar of the community, helping at many charitable events and is totally different from her brother.

Although not strictly asked about at talks, I felt the following amusing anecdotes might be of interest at this point. Between 1992 and 1995 I was a member of the newly formed "Inspectorate Department" of Sussex police. This was set up by the Chief Constable to check on the efficiency of the force and to also highlight elements of good practice across the numerous geographical policing districts

My area of responsibility was uniform policing aspects, such as inspecting sample prisoner custody records, search authorisations, and similar procedures. One day, I was at Eastbourne police station and was expected to audit the recovered vehicles which were stored in the rear car park. I checked the register against the actual cars parked there. I noticed there was a discrepancy with one car missing and no explanation in the register.

I decided I needed to query this with the young sergeant responsible for the local procedure. "Ah" he said, as I pointed out what I had discovered, "I hoped you might not have noticed that one".

"So where is the car now?" I asked, presuming it had been reclaimed by the rightful owner and the register had not been endorsed.

"It was stolen out of the rear yard, Guv" explained the rather embarrassed officer. "Have you discovered it yet?" I asked. "Oh yes. It's at the foot of Beachy Head where someone has dumped it" came the embarrassed reply.

It turned out that the problem of poor security at the police station had been raised many times before. Anyone could wander into the rear yard at any time and quite clearly had done so on this occasion. Suffice to say that after our report was published Eastbourne police station suddenly had shiny new electronic gates fitted.

Rye in East Sussex is without doubt my favourite town in the whole of the police force area. It has links with smuggling going back centuries and is home to The Mermaid Inn. This building was once associated with the infamous Hawkhurst Gang, a notorious criminal organisation throughout southeast England from 1735 until 1749.

The gang was based in the "Oak and Ivy Inn", Hawkhurst. But their secondary headquarters was The Mermaid Inn, where they would sit with their loaded weapons on the table seemingly immune from prosecution. Many local legends are based on the alleged network of tunnels built by the gang.

One evening a colleague and I were sitting in another of Rye's atmospheric pubs. Two locals were at the bar stools a little further away, but we could clearly hear what they were saying.

One of the men began chuckling to himself and his friend asked him what was so amusing. "Well" he said, "Them buggers won't be returning to nick my logs any time soon" he said,

"Why is that then?" asked his friend. "Well I've hollowed out some of the logs and filled them with gun powder from my shot gun cartridges. When they chuck them on their fires in their bloody caravans they're in for a shock!"

Chapter 10

The usual suspects: Identification parades

A crime has been committed, let's say a burglary at a country pub. Four witnesses have seen a man going up the fire escape at the rear of the building. About twenty minutes later the man was seen to walk down the fire escape, obviously concealing items under his jacket. He kept looking around suspiciously and got into his car and drove away quickly.

Each witnesses recorded his car number plate and they all said they would be able to recognize him again. A suspect had then been detained who had nothing incriminating in his car and vehemently denied he was the person responsible, although he matched the description. We then needed to test the witness's powers of recognition with an Identification Parade (or line up).

At the time such a parade had to consist of at least eight people (in addition to the suspect) who, so far as possible, resembled the suspect in the following areas:

- age,
- height,
- general appearance   _and_
- similar position in life (whatever that meant. I never fully understood this point)

It's all to ensure fairness for the suspect. Nowadays there are more hi-tech ways of showing witnesses potential suspects with video clips. lap top computers etc. But the more traditional method was the good old "Line Up" or ID Parade.

As a uniform Inspector it was one of my jobs to organise and run quite a few of these across Sussex. How difficult do you think it would be to get hold of eight other men to help out on a parade like this at 7pm on a wet Tuesday night? Even by offering to pay each of them £10 for their trouble it was an uphill struggle. However, in the end we managed it.

The parade was to be run at Horsham police station where the suspect was under arrest. It was 7pm and I had despatched officers to Horsham railway station who had "invited" various commuters to help us run the parade. Whilst selecting the men to invite, I had only gone by the brief descriptions from the witnesses in their written statements.

I had overlooked one vital descriptive fact we will come to in a moment. It was a fact about which I was blissfully unaware when I had tasked them. When I eventually walked down to the custody block where the suspect was being detained, I had quite a shock. I entered the suspect's cell and had a moment of blinding realisation. I had asked for volunteers to be selected on age and general appearance.

When I looked at the man sitting in the cell, I realised he must have spent a lot of time "pumping iron" in the gym and, no doubt, took steroids on a regular basis. He looked like a weight lifter and not at all similar to my volunteers sitting patiently in the police station parade room. He appeared to have no neck, his head seeming to sit directly on his incredibly broad, muscular shoulders.

In fact, none of my willing volunteers had a physique anything like the suspect. Many were particularly puny. So, what to do to keep the defence solicitor happy and make the procedure acceptable in a court of law at a later date? I really wanted the parade to go ahead that evening, not least because I had four women witnesses sitting patiently in separate rooms. They had the man they saw that afternoon fresh in their memories.

Are they suitable ?

What I decided to do was to ask my eight selected volunteers to sit down on chairs. I raided the cell block bedding store and placed white sheets around their shoulders. This overcame the obvious discrepancy with the physique.

Amazingly the defence solicitor seemed happy with my proposal and my weight lifting suspect seemed happy also as it seemed to give him a better chance of maybe getting away with it.

I went and told the witnesses not to burst out laughing when they entered the parade room. I said they would see nine men looking as if they were waiting for a hair dresser. In the end this unusual method was successful.

All four witnesses picked out the suspect with very little hesitation. This, despite the fact that after every witness left the room he was given the chance to move to a different position in the line-up.

"Anyone for a short back and sides?"

Like I had to do with sheets and volunteers sitting down

I shall never forget his final comment when I asked him if he had anything to say about the way I had conducted the four parades. And I quote: "They must all be mistaken. I never went near that pub today" said the professional burglar, who received a lengthy custodial sentence when the case went to court.

My all-time favourite incident involving an identification parade appeared in the Daily Telegraph obituary of a well know Glasgow defence solicitor named Joe Beltrami. Joe had died in February 2015. Unless you are a hardened Glasgow villain, you have probably never heard of Beltrami. He was Scotland's best-known and most controversial criminal defence lawyer. The headline to his obituary read: "*Glasgow lawyer who defended 350 clients accused of murder, saving 12 of them from the gallows*". Within the obituary it mentioned the following which has often brought a smile to my lips:

"*His (Beltrami's) most unusual client was Hercules the Bear, who went missing in the Western Isles in 1980. The bear's owner, a former wrestling champion, was charged with failing to keep a wild animal under control.*

Beltrami got the charges dropped after he proved that Hercules was a working animal and threatened to demand an identity parade involving six other bears if the charges went ahead".

Hercules had been at liberty for twenty four days in September 1980. When located he was shot with a tranquilliser dart and returned to his owner, wrestler Andy Robbins. Subsequently, Robbins had been charged with failing to keep a wild animal under control.

When a suspect has agreed to attend an identification parade they are expected to turn up looking similar in appearance to when they were bailed. I was due to run a parade in Brighton police station for a serious offence of kidnapping and had gone to great lengths to collect together a number of men of a similar age, height and general appearance to be my parade volunteers

The suspect answered his bail with his solicitor and, when I went to meet him, I realised in the intervening few weeks he had grown quite a luxuriant moustache. This was a facial feature none of my volunteers possessed.

Rather than postpone the parade as all witnesses were present, it was suggested I might like to ask for the services of the make-up artist at the nearby Brighton Theatre Royal. Luckily the person was still at the theatre and readily agreed to walk across to the police station. I sought approval from the defence solicitor and my ten available volunteers and this was given.

I delayed the start time of the parade so the make-up artist could weave her magic on the ten rather bemused men in the waiting room. The classic way to attach a fake theatrical moustache with reliable staying power is by using spirit gum, a glue-like adhesive meant for application to the face. Spirit gum, however, can be messy to work with and painful to remove but, ever the professional, the make- up artist wanted to do the right thing, so spirit gum it was. The parade began with all men sporting similar moustaches to the suspect.

Not having used the parade room at Brighton before, I had not appreciated how hot it became after about fifteen minutes due to the spot lights shining down on the men. The one- way mirrored glass meant that myself, the solicitor and the witnesses remained cool, in stark contrast to the men on the other side of the screen.

After the first witness had examined the parade, the suspect was allowed to change his place in the "line up". It was only then that I walked back into the room with the parade and the heat really hit me.

As I turned to leave, the suspect called out to me "Here mate, I don't want to worry you, but one of your stooges is moulting".

I turned around to see that one of the volunteers was standing there with half his moustache dangling down, held only by a thread of rapidly melting glue. We quickly had it reattached. Sadly, for the life of me, I can not remember if the suspect was picked out or not.

At about the same time (1997) another identification case made the newspaper   headlines and also used the services of a make-up artist. However, it involved a far more dramatic and controversial "change of appearance".

South Yorkshire police were widely criticised after it emerged the faces of white men were painted by a make-up artist in an attempt to make them look like the non white defendant at an identification parade. Their hands, however, were left white. South Yorkshire said they could not find any volunteers in Sheffield to appear on the parade that looked like the suspect who was 6ft 3, weighed 16 stone and was black and bald. They had contacted police in Bradford, Leeds and Newcastle for alternative volunteers, but failed to find any.

After hearing details of the identification parade in pre-trial submissions, the judge ruled the defendant should be discharged. The judge said: "It's a farce when the faces of white men are painted black for an identity parade. Ethnic origin is not only to do with colour, it is to do with other features

---

Talks experience   I need to stress that there are more technological methods available today to allow witnesses to view potential suspects. The reason I say this is that at one talk in Burgess Hill I noticed a woman wince when I showed a photograph of the old fashioned "line up".

After the talk had finished, I went and sat by her and asked her about that particular slide. She said that it had brought back disturbing memories of when she had worked in a building society. One day, a man approached her position and, thrusting a plastic bag across the counter, he demanded she fill it with cash as he had a gun and would shoot her if she refused.

Understandably, she complied with the robber's demand, only pressing the alarm as he ran out of the branch. She went on to say that the man was caught almost immediately and she was asked to attend an identification parade. She recalled that walking along the line of men, so close to the man who had scared her so badly, was as traumatic as the actual robbery.

Chapter 11

Stories from the Clink (prisons and prisoners)

Question: *Which country in the developed world has the highest proportion of its citizens in prison?*

Answer: *The USA has a total population of 328 million with a prison population of a staggering 2.3 million people. Just out of interest the USA has about 25% of the worlds entire prison population.*

The UK has about 84,000 people locked up at Her Majesty's pleasure at any one time. If we had the same proportion of the population as the USA that figure would be about 530,000 prisoners. To be brutally honest, we can't really afford the 84,000 we already have.

I attended a talk once and the speaker was a retired prison governor. He told us that when he went to his first prison in a managerial capacity he was startled to find that the dog handlers received more per day to feed their animals than the catering manager received to feed each inmate.

Some of the people I've arrested or come into contact with over the years have ended up behind bars. Some have received fines or non-custodial sentences. However, I've also visited a number of different prison establishments (in a professional capacity, of course) and some even looked like the building portrayed in the TV comedy "Porridge" with Ronnie Barker as the old lag, Norman Stanley Fletcher, or just Fletch

While I mention Porridge, I always remember one of the funniest scenes in that first series.

Lennie Godber (Richard Beckensale) is meeting his new cell mate Fletcher (Ronnie Barker) for the first time at HMP Slade.

"I'm only here due to tragic circumstances" says new boy Godber.

"Which were?" asks Fletcher.   "I got caught" replies Godber.

During its three-years on the BBC, the prison sitcom recruited an army of fans and introduced a cast that included David Jason and Peter Vaughan. Vaughan, terrified fellow inmates as the villainous Harry 'Grouty' Grout and went on to enjoy a late final career flourish in the cult TV series Game of Thrones. He was a veteran tough guy of screen and stage and died, aged 93, in December 2016 .

Talks experience I was giving my second Policeman's Lot talk at Mannings Heath village hall, West Sussex in 2015 and showed a slide of a scene from Porridge to introduce a section relating to prisons.

All of a sudden a lady called out, "He was outside this morning, you know". Rather surprised, I asked "Who was?"" and she replied "Grouty was in the road outside taking his daily exercise".

It turned out that actor Peter Vaughan actually lived in their village and, on a regular basis, could be seen taking his daily walk. They told me he would always wear shorts and a luminous jacket so he could be seen as his eyesight was less than perfect. Sadly, I never got to see or meet him, as he died shortly afterwards.

Coincidentally, a new development of houses has been built near his former home. It has been called Vaughan Close. I suppose "Grouty Close" might not have sounded so attractive on the sales brochure !!

Let's start with a prison close to my home in West Sussex : HMP Ford. This is near Littlehampton and the lovely river side town of Arundel.

It's a category D establishment with the emphasis on "resettlement" and was converted to an open prison in 1960 after life as a Fleet Air Arm base.

Members of the public (and some police officers too) are often confused about the meaning of the various categories of prisons in the UK. There are four categories, A,B,C,and D. According to the Gov.UK site   In England and Wales, prisoners are categorised based on:

- risk of escape
- harm to the public, if they were to escape
- threat to the control and stability of a prison

- *Category A:*
These are high security prisons. They house male prisoners who, if they were to escape, pose the most threat to the public, the police or national security.
These establishments are sometimes called "High security" prisons.
They include the likes of;
   - HMP Belmarsh.
   - HMP Frankland.
   - HMP Long Lartin.

Category B: These prisons are either local or training prisons. Local prisons house prisoners that are taken directly from court in the local area (sentenced or on remand, in other words they are awaiting their trial), and training prisons which hold long-term and high-security prisoners. Such as;

   - HMP Lewes,
   - Parkstone
   - Brixton

Category C: These prisons are training and resettlement prisons; most prisoners are located in a category C. They provide prisoners with the opportunity to develop their own skills so they can find work and resettle back into the community on release. These include:

- HMP Coldingly (Surrey)
- HMP Dartmoor
- HMP Pentonville

And finally

Category D: Open prisons

These prisons have minimal security and allow eligible prisoners to spend most of their day away from the prison on licence to carry out work, education or for other resettlement purposes. Open prisons only house prisoners that have been risk-assessed and deemed suitable for open conditions. These include:

- HMP Ford
- HMP Leyhill
- HMP North Sea Camp

It was rather ironic that at the time of my visit in 1983 HMP Ford did not accept offenders with a conviction for either sexual offences or arson. I say this as on January 1st 2011 specialist prison officers in riot gear quelled a riot by around forty inmates who had burned some of the prison buildings to the ground.

Some previous illustrious guests at Ford have included; Disgraced former cabinet minister Jonathan Aitken who also spent time at HMP Belmarsh before being sent to Ford.

It has also played host to a clutch of upper-class inmates in the past, including the Guinness fraudsters Ernest Saunders, Gerald Ronson and Anthony Parnes.

George Best, the professional footballer was an inmate at Ford for three months after a drink- driving conviction. Contrary to my early beliefs, Best never actually turned out for the prison football team, even though for many years I had told groups that he had. He refused to put himself in a position where a photographer could ridicule him. On release from HMP Ford George is quoted as saying: "I had tears in my eyes the day I left Ford...people talk about it as a holiday camp...but in many respects it's even better!" But there again his most celebrated quip was supposed to have been: "In 1969 I gave up women and alcohol...it was the worst 20 minutes of my life!"

Another former inmate of Ford was Charles Brocket; otherwise known as Charles Ronald George Nall-Cain, 3rd Baron Brocket. He served half of his five year sentence for insurance fraud after claiming £4.3 million for three Ferraris and a Maserati which he alleged had been stolen.

Brocket was an inmate in no less than seven different prisons and was transferred to Ford in 1996 after being stabbed in another establishment. When I looked into his case I found he was knifed and slashed across the hands and face with a razor by other prisoners. As a "celebrity" inmate, other prisoners would stare at him or be simply curious. But others would "eye him up" to see what they could possibly get from him; be it money or favours they thought he can do for them on the outside. Many years later Brocket wrote a bestselling autobiography and in 2004 appeared in the third series of "I'm A Celebrity... Get Me Out Of Here!" Among his camp mates were former Sex Pistol John Lydon and Katie Price (then still going by the name of Jordan) and Peter Andre, whom she went on to marry.

Talks experience When I showed a slide of a rather dashing Charles Brocket in Savile Row suit at one talk, a lady called out "Oh poor Charlie", which threw me a little. I asked her if she knew Lord Brocket personally and she said she did. She went on to tell the group that many years before she used to be his nanny when the family were abroad for the skiing season. I asked her why she had said "Poor Charlie" and she replied that he must have been put up to the insurance scam as he wasn't, in her words, "the sharpest knife in the box" and would never have dreamt up such an elaborate plan on his own!

My visit to HMP Ford was in the mid-1980s as part of a police management course. Myself and a colleague were meeting with the Governor in his office. Suddenly, there was a knock on the office door and in walked a "Trustie" (a prisoner with an arm band showing he had more responsibility than others.)

I remember he was an incredibly dapper man of around fifty years of age and I was quite taken aback when he spoke with a very cultured voice. "Excuse me gentlemen", he said, "May I get you some tea or coffee?" After he left the room, I asked the Governor what the man was in prison for.

He smiled and replied "Let's just say he's a former Inland Revenue Tax Inspector who went a bit off the rails and kept some of the money back for himself!"

On the next visit we went to HMP Coldingly near Woking in Surrey. This was opened in 1969 as a Category B training prison focussing on the resettlement of prisoners.

121

It provided a framework to support prisoners willing to work hard and is much more modern than HMP Ford. It was a fascinating visit as it had very productive metal workshops. When we visited they had won a large order for metal road sign supports which crumpled on impact and were said to be much safer than the older, tubular structures.

But I couldn't get over their other speciality: manufacturing light weight aluminium ladders of all things in a prison! I resisted the urge to ask the prison officers how they tested the ladders.

We were walking from one prison block to another and I couldn't help noticing a very muscular, well-tanned prisoner tending rose bushes near the smoking area. He was wielding a set of what looked like sharp secateurs which I thought was rather dangerous in a prison.

When I mentioned this to one of the prison staff, he asked me if I had recognised him. I hadn't, but it turned out this gentleman, who was so proud of his roses, had been the Kray twin's "Enforcer" or a muscle-man for the notorious East London gangsters. The man was a "Trustie" prisoner and was scheduled for release in the near future, so he was allowed to use the secateurs.

The man's name was Tony Lambrianou. He was released in 1983 and died in 2004. He had served 15 years for various horrendous crimes of violence, not least being concerned with the murder by Reggie Kray of a villain called Jack "The Hat" McVitie in 1967.

The unfortunate McVitie's body was never found, although there were plenty of rumours circulating around the East End of London at the time. Some said it was concreted into the foundations of a building in the City. Others maintained it had been put into the furnaces of Bankside power station.

However, in June 1991 Tony Lambrianou gave an interview to the now defunct News of the World. In it he admitted that he buried Jack's body in (of all places) Gravesend. It was placed at the bottom of a pre-dug grave and the official resident's coffin was placed on top.

Talks Experience At a talk in Saltdean in 2013, a lady who was originally from the East End of London, came over and told me she had often seen Jack McVitie walking down her road in the early 1960s.

She said he had a habit of taking "pot-shots" at people he didn't like. She recalled being told to hide at the rear of her house if he was about. If shots were heard out in the street all the children would go out to search for spent cartridge cases on the pavement. "He was really mad you know" she told me.

Finally, the last prison visit was the most bizarre of all. It was at HMP Chelmsford in Essex. I was walking along one of the landings with a prison officer and had just turned a corner when I literally bumped into a prisoner coming out of his cell. I was amazed to watch him bend forward and lock his cell door with a key. He put the key in his trouser pocket, turned and carried on walking along the landing.

I asked the prison officer if I had been hallucinating, but he assured me that the prisoner could only lock the door from outside and couldn't get out once back inside his cell. He was a Trustie and would be released in the near future.

I was rather taken aback and asked if I could catch up with the prisoner and have a chat. When I reached him, I asked him why he had locked his cell door. It turned out he had been given a couple of pet budgies and he had let them out for a fly around in his cell. He was afraid someone might open the door and they might escape, as he wanted to take them home with him on his imminent release! His final, throw away comment to me was priceless. "You can't be too careful in here mate- there's a lot of crooks about you know!"

So, next time you watch old re-runs of "Porridge" on TV think of some of the real life characters who inhabit our prisons.

They are from all backgrounds and walks of life, be they disgraced titled gentlemen, professional footballers or ex-MPs to name just a few.

An early photograph at a talk in Lewes showing some "props"

Whilst on the subject of prisons and criminals, in my second police talk (The Beat goes on) I speak about running a course for the Abu Dhabi police when I was seconded to the National Police College at Bramshill, Hampshire. In 2005 I was sent to work with the Abu Dhabi police and ran a course on Health and Safety (no doubt a subject dear to the heart of many reading this today!) I had created the course, produced the handouts, all the Powerpoint slides to accompany the week long course and, importantly, the final exam which the students would need to pass. On arrival at the military style base in the desert the temperature had touched 35C degrees and I was very relieved to find my classroom for the week was air conditioned.

The room had been set up for me with a large horseshoe of chairs, screen and projector. There was a knock on the door and I called out "Come in", at which point twenty five young men, all sergeants and all dressed identically wandered in and took their seats. I was feeling a little nervous but commenced the first session with a cheery "Good morning, my name is Inspector Neil Sadler from the British Police Staff College and I am very pleased to meet you all."

I got absolutely no reaction. It became abundantly clear that none of my students spoke a word of English! Sadly, nobody had thought to tell me this fact as I had prepared everything in English.

Whilst I was standing there getting more panic-stricken as the minutes ticked by, there was another knock on the classroom door and in walked a distinguished gentleman in full flowing Arabic robes and head wear.

"Good morning Mr Neil", the newcomer said, "I am Mohammed and I will be your translator for this week". If you have been unfortunate enough to need to work through an interpreter it can be rather frustrating, as everything is done at half speed.

Progress was slowed done even more by Mohammed telling me every now and again that the students needed a smoke break. So, they trooped out for a ten minute chat and a puff. Off we went again for another half hour when Mohammed advised me the students needed a coffee break. Finally, a little later, I was told the students now needed a prayer break. So, as you can imagine the morning went very slowly

That afternoon we were discussing the potential dangers of various police roles and the discussion came round to guns and other firearms. There was a noticeable change in the atmosphere in the room. I couldn't for the life of me fathom out what I had said or done to cause this. When we next had one of our numerous breaks, I took Mohammed to one side and asked him about this. "Well Mr Neil," he replied, "In your country I assume you are tasked with different jobs at your briefing?" I agreed that was the case.

He continued, "Did you notice everyone looking at Abdul when you were talking about gun safety?" I had indeed noticed everyone look over towards Abdul, who had been sitting in the corner of the classroom, not far from my desk. "Well in our country Abdul has a very special job to perform. When he goes to the briefing he is told if there is a prisoner in the cells and if there is, it his job to go down and shoot them!" Unknown to me I had been lecturing to the country's chief executioner, on the subject of health and safety of all things!

As you can imagine I made very sure that Abdul received extremely good marks in the final exam, but I was very aware of him eyeing me up and down to gauge the best place to shoot me should he fail the course.

After another talk, a lady confided in me that she had been a hospital nurse many years before.

She was starting her night shift and was told by the off-going nurse to keep an eye on "Albert" the elderly gentleman in the bed by the window, as he was "special".

Quite naturally, she asked what made him "special" and was told that he was Albert Pierrepoint, the former UK hangman / executioner and that she had better not make any mistakes with him.

Pierrepoint was also a publican at The Help the Poor Struggler pub in Oldham as the role of executioner was only a part time occupation. Diminutive, always immaculately-dressed and with a penchant for cigars, boxing and coin tricks, Pierrepoint became a Licensee in 1946.

Some claimed a sign in the pub read 'No Hanging Around the Bar', although he always denied that. The role of executioner ran in his family, as his father and uncle were hangmen also. Young Albert was born in 1905 and he was just nine-years-old when he seemed set on following in his father's line of work. At school, when asked to write down what he would like to be when he grew up, Albert wrote the following; "When I leave school I should like to be a public executioner like my Dad is, because it needs a steady man with good hands like my Dad and my Uncle Tom and I shall be the same."

From 1931 until his resignation in 1956, he carried out over 400 executions and taught his methods to foreign colleagues. He had a long career, executing some of the most high-profile criminals of his day and putting several Nazi war criminals to death following the Belsen concentration camp trials. His "customers" had included John George Haigh, the Acid bath murderer who worked out of a workshop in Leopold Rd, Crawley and was convicted of five murders. Also, the last woman to be executed in Britain was Ruth

Ellis. She was a model and nightclub hostess and was convicted of murdering her lover, David Blakely.

In February 1956 Pierrepoint resigned following a dispute over payment. He was paid a derisory amount after travelling to a prison for an execution, only to be told that an appeal had been allowed .

The death penalty was abolished in Great Britain in 1965. In his autobiography Pierrepoint made a startling confession. He wrote: "Capital punishment is said to be a deterrent. I cannot agree. There have been murders since the beginning of time, and we shall go on looking for deterrents until the end of time. All the men and women whom I have faced at that final moment convince me that in what I have done I have not prevented a single murder."

After years of putting criminals to death, Albert seemed to be at peace with the idea that he had not made an iota of difference. Just as a post script, on July 15th 1953 notorious British serial killer John Christie was about to be executed at Pentonville prison.
Immediately before he was hanged and with his hands tied behind his back, he said to Pierrepoint that his nose itched. The executioner is said to have leaned forward and told Christie, "It won't bother you for long!"

Finally, in this chapter, you may wonder why there are so many people locked up in UK prisons. It's because some of them do daft things and then wonder why they get caught. The following letter appeared in a national newspaper and I think sums up this hypothesis perfectly.

Received with thanks

SIR – Some years ago, one of my Suffolk rural churches was burgled. Altar cross and candles were taken, and the offertory box emptied.

The thieves were soon apprehended, for they had signed the visitors' book (Letters, April 22), leaving their home address.

Canon John Simpson
Publow, Somerset

Chapter 12

Come fly with me (airport policing)

In mid-1988 I was transferred to Gatwick airport police division and appointed the Inspector in charge of "D" section. On my first night shift I was due to meet the man I was to replace who had secured a different role at the airport.

After an initial introduction in the Inspector's office, my colleague suggested we went down the corridor to the night shift briefing where I could be introduced to my new team. Bearing in mind I had just left mid Sussex where I had been responsible for just two sergeants and twelve constables, I was rather shocked as we entered the Briefing Room.

Firstly, there was standing room only as all the chairs around the enormous table were occupied. There was a mix of men and women, but it was the sheer number of bodies that startled me. I said to my colleague "Why have we kept the preceding shift on duty?" He replied "We haven't. All this lot are yours!"

I would estimate there were about thirty to forty officers in the room. I asked the other Inspector how on earth he managed to remember all their names. "I don't" he replied, "There is such a turnover of staff it is almost impossible to recall everyone's names"

So started a very interesting, varied and enjoyable few years with a superb bunch of officers who, whilst always acting in a professional manner, had a penchant for fun and the odd practical joke.

Forty seven million passengers pass through Gatwick airport each year. Well they did before the global pandemic of 2020. But as they hurried through on their way to check in and security gates, most were scarcely aware of what is happening around them or behind the scenes.

During my thirty years as a Sussex police officer, I served at the airport on two separate occasions. Firstly, way back in 1981 as a Constable and then between 1988-90 as an Inspector and Acting Chief inspector. I have to be honest and say that I found it a fascinating and, at times, quite exciting place to work.

Without doubt I was involved in things at the airport I would never experience anywhere else in Sussex. Some events were even stranger than fiction.

I suspect most people have experienced the joys and frustrations of passing through a modern airport. You may have seen the airline check in staff, the cleaners, the aircrew in their fancy uniforms and the often frazzled, security staff asking you to remove your belts, shoes and anything else concealed in your pockets.

You may also have spotted the uniformed and armed police officers patrolling the terminal concourse or departure gates. They may have been wearing their bulky bullet proof vests and carrying Heckler and Koch MP5 sub machine guns. Seeing these officers patrolling the terminals for passenger reassurance is one thing; but have you ever wondered what weird and wonderful things they get called to deal with in an eight-hour shift?

Let me start with a very brief history lesson. Long before we all took off from Gatwick airport for Ibiza and the Algarve the area was better known in horse racing circles. Since 1891 there had been a race track, stables, good transport links and even a dedicated railway station connecting the viewing stands to the platforms.

When World War 1 began the War Office requisitioned Aintree racecourse, near Liverpool and the famous Grand National horse race needed to look for a new, temporary home. Gatwick had space to replicate exactly the Grand National distance of 4 miles and 856 yards plus the required twenty- nine fences. The only difference, for those horse racing buffs, was that it was a right handed course, not left handed like Aintree. The current Satellite terminal's departure gates at the South Terminal would be right in the centre of the racetrack.

In 1918 the Grand National was won by Poethlyn, ridden by a jockey named Ernie Piggott, a name well known in horse racing circles in the early part of the twentieth century and also the latter part, as he was the grand-father of a certain Lester Piggott.

Interestingly, when the Grand National returned to Aintree the following year, 1919, Ernie won it again on the very same horse; no wonder he was Champion jockey three times. Lester was Champion Jockey eleven times in his career and at 5ft 8 inches tall his nick name was "The Long Fellow" or more commonly known as "The house wife's choice"

Horse racing continued at Gatwick race track, with the airport growing around it during the 1930s and 40s. The final race meeting was held in 1946. Everything was demolished with the exception of the bandstand. This was taken down and re-assembled in the centre of the local New Town, Crawley.

Subsequently, the Air Ministry approved commercial flights from Gatwick in 1933 and the very first terminal, the Beehive, was built in 1935. The building is still there today but quite some way from the current airport perimeter. You get a very good view of it from the London to Brighton train

Charter flights at Gatwick were encouraged by the Ministry of Aviation and many of the new "bucket and spade" foreign destinations were served by Gatwick. British Caledonian (BCal) became Gatwick's dominant scheduled and charter airline during the 1970s. This period also coincided with Sussex Police taking over responsibility for policing the airport with an upsurge in domestic and international terrorism.

From 1974 onwards many young single police officers were posted to the new airport division, most against their will as they had just completed their two year probationary period and were looking forward to developing their skills locally, where they had put down roots. Not surprisingly, many a romance blossomed between young police officers and air hostesses and check-in ground staff and many marriages followed.

If you are of a certain age you will probably remember a fateful night in 1969 when Gatwick Airport featured on the international news, sadly for all the wrong reasons. On 5 January 1969 at 1.35am on that Sunday morning, the Gatwick area was affected by patches of dense freezing fog. A Boeing 727 of Ariana Afghan Airlines arriving from Frankfurt airport descended below its correct glide slope as it approached the airport from the east.

As it passed over the hamlet of Fernhill onthe Surrey/Sussex border, it hit trees and roofs, began to roll and crashed into a field south of Fernhill Lane, about a mile and a half (2.4 km) short of the runway. It also collided with a large detached house, which was demolished and then caught fire.

Forty-eight passengers and crew died, and two adult occupants of the house were also killed. A baby in the house survived with minor injuries. By some miracle, the captain, first officer, flight engineer and eleven passengers also survived

A major incident was declared and police from Surrey and Sussex rushed to the scene. Two officers were searching through the debris of the demolished house and heard the cries of a baby which turned out to be a little girl named Beverley Jones. The local newspaper printed a story entitled "The miracle escape of baby Beverley (6th January 1969). Exactly fifty years later one of those police officers, Keith Simmonds, was reunited with Beverley and her rescued Teddy bear which had featured on the front page of many newspapers in 1969.

The demon drink; alcohol and altitude don't mix

The Golden Age of air travel was where people used to actually dress up for "the event" of flying. It's a bit different today and there is a lot less respect for airline staff and other travelling passengers.

According to a BBC investigation for Panorama (2017) arrests of passengers suspected of being drunk at UK airports and on flights have risen by 50% in a year. A total of 387 people were arrested between February 2016 and February 2017 - up from 255 the previous year.

Meanwhile, more than half of cabin crew who responded to a survey said they had witnessed disruptive drunken passenger behaviour at UK airports. A former cabin crew manager with Virgin, Ally Murphy, quit her job after 14 years and told Panorama: "People just see us as barmaids in the sky."

Even though entering an aircraft when drunk or being drunk on an aircraft is a criminal offence, with a maximum sentence of two years' imprisonment, some people can't resist the five pints of lager at 5 a.m before their flight to the sun. The Civil Aviation Authority reported a 600% increase in disruptive passenger incidents in the UK between 2012 and 2016 with "most involving alcohol".

Probably one of my most satisfying shifts at Gatwick was in the early 1990's as a uniform Patrol Inspector. It was quite late and some of my officers were called to a departure gate on the Satellite in the

South Terminal. The captain of a delayed night flight to Ibiza wanted our assistance.

I arrived shortly afterwards and went on board with a couple of officers. All we could hear as we approached the aircraft was raucous singing and a spot of drunken swearing.

The chief stewardess told me there was a group of young men causing a commotion and the captain wanted **the two ringleaders** off loaded before he would take off. I approached the two lads who had been pointed out to me and asked them, very politely, to come with me. As the two stood up reluctantly, about six others also stood and declared that if their mates were being off- loaded then so were they.

As the eight rowdy young men started to leave the plane after gathering up their cabin baggage, all the other passengers cheered and clapped, no doubt relived their family flight to the sun would now be a whole lot quieter.

As the aircraft door slammed shut the main ringleader turned to me and in a slurred voice said the immortal words "It's not fair. We should be in Ibiza upsetting the Spanish police, not you lot!".

I told him it was people like him and his friends that made me feel proud to be British. They were surprised when they asked where their replacement flight was and I said, "What replacement flight?" as we all marched landside to collect their off- loaded luggage and wish them a speedy trip home.

I am not implying that all groups of young men (and women) in high spirits would be guaranteed to cause serious problems when in mid- air. But there have been a depressing number of such incidents recorded in recent years. Sometimes the issue is the effect of alcohol on people at 35,000 feet altitude or the fact they consume excessive amounts of alcohol in flight either lawfully or by swigging duty free booze purchased at the airport shop.

The first ever recorded case of "Air Rage" was in 1947 on a flight from Havana to Miami, when a drunk man assaulted another passenger and a flight attendant. A couple of examples involving well-known people demonstrates a continuance of the problem in the twenty first century.

In 2002 US. guitarist Peter Buck from group REM was in the First Class cabin on a BA flight from Seattle to Heathrow. After flight attendants refused to serve him a 16th glass of wine he became disorderly. He also tore up a "Yellow card" warning notice handed to him by the captain and then sprayed two flight attendants with yoghurt.

After his arrest he attributed his actions to the interaction of the alcohol and pre-flight sleeping pills and claimed to recall nothing of the incident.
A jury at Isleworth Crown Court, near Heathrow, accepted his explanation that he was not truly responsible for his actions.

 He had employed the seldom used defence of non-insane Automatism. This means he was not aware of his actions when doing something which is an illegal act

The following year actor and former Premiership footballer Vinnie Jones was fined £1,100 and sentenced to 80 hours community service for his actions on a Virgin Airways flight from Heathrow to Tokyo.

A fellow passenger had told Jones to stop annoying a female passenger. Jones slapped the man ten times and yelled, "Don't you know who I am?" This attracted the attention of flight crew whom Jones told to "Go away and make coffee like you are paid to do".

He also loudly informed them he could have them all killed for a mere £3,000.

As an aside, back in the mid 1990s I used to take my children to watch Wimbledon AFC at Selhurst Park. This was in the heady days when they were a Premiership club. Who should be their captain at the time but Vinnie Jones. We often took bets on how long it would take him to get himself sent off for one piece of violent play or another.

Clearly, even sitting in First or Business Class does not guarantee a peaceful flight. Neither is nationality or status in life. It is not always drunken stag and hen parties that cause trouble, exemplified by the odd case of a very disruptive Russian gentleman.

In 2019 Dr Vadim Bondar, an anaesthetist, had been drinking rum on a flight from Bangkok to Moscow when he became "extremely aggressive" and had to be restrained by fellow passengers. Terrified passengers were forced to tie the drunken doctor to a seat to stop him from opening the emergency exit at 33,000ft. He caused terror on the Aeroflot flight and became "extremely aggressive", according to local media. When he tried to physically open the exit door, a Norwegian traveller led the way in tackling him before Russians came to his aid. Bondar later apologised to passengers on Russian TV, saying: "First of all, there were no demands for hijacking or anything." So that's OK then!

And we think litigation has gone too far in the West? Some time later Dr Bonder had the nerve to say he would be talking to his lawyers about his treatment on the flight.

Another passenger you would certainly not want to sit next to on a flight is Chloe Haines, a 26 year old from High Wycombe. She was a passenger who tried to storm the cockpit of a Jet2 aircraft in June 2019 flight after consuming a large quantity of alcohol. The flight to Dalaman in Turkey, was forced to return to Stansted Airport after the pilot issued a hijack alert.

RAF fighters responded to the mayday call. This caused a sonic boom over the area. Haines had to be restrained by passengers and crew. Jet2 later fined her £85,000 and banned her from flying with the airline for life. She subsequently appeared at Chelmsford Crown Court and pleaded guilty to assault and endangering the safety of an aircraft. For her trouble she was sentenced to two years imprisonment

"When is a bomb not a bomb?"

In the late 1980s Gatwick airport was on high alert due to the activities of various terrorist groups including Irish extremism and Arabic terrorism. This all necessitated extra armed officers as major international airports were viewed as possible terrorist targets.

You might recall that on Wednesday 21 December 1988, Pan Am flight 103 took off from Heathrow for JFK airport in New York. It was named Clipper Maid of the Seas.

Whilst flying over the border between England and Scotland, the aircraft was destroyed by a bomb, killing all 243 passengers and 16 crew members. What is often forgotten is that eleven people in the town of Lockerbie itself, in southern Scotland were also killed, as large sections of the plane fell on and around the town.
This brought the total fatalities to 270. As a result, the event has been named by the media as the Lockerbie Bombing.

It was against this back ground that I found myself posted to Gatwick airport division, responsible for a small army of officers, half of whom were armed with pistols and Heckler and Koch MP5 sub machine guns.

A problem frequently encountered was of passengers forgetting to pick up a suitcase, briefcase etc in their hurry to catch their flight. Or on their return journey home, getting a bit befuddled by the hustle and bustle of a busy international airport. Everyone was reminded that unattended bags could be dangerous and you will still hear at airports the warning "Unattended bags will be removed and may be destroyed".

All Inspectors were trained in procedures for X-raying such unattended, suspicious bags. This meant that the military bomb disposal teams didn't need to be called on every occasion. It also meant we could clear a suspect bag quickly and open up that area of the airport as fast as possible This aspect was something for which the Terminal Duty Manager was very thankful.

One such abandoned bag incident arose and I went to check on progress. I found that all the necessary checks had been done, loudspeaker calls put out to notify the owner of the small suit case and, so far, no one had claimed it.

I called for the X-ray equipment and had the area cordoned off, as there would be potentially dangerous X-rays pinging around very soon. The pictures which normally emerged from these machines were notoriously "fuzzy" and hard to decipher. However, on this occasion I saw what clearly looked to me like the component parts of a bomb.

There was a small clock, wires and the dark outline of what looked like sticks of gelignite with wires coming out of the top of each "stick". This all appeared to be horribly realistic. I had the whole area closed down and called the nearest Bomb Disposal team.

My X- ray photo was examined by the expert, dressed appropriately in bomb proof suit, helmet and visor. "I can see now why you called us Inspector", said the Warrant Officer, which made me slightly more comfortable about the whole affair. He then said words I shall never forget. "I will take the case away and disrupt it". The item was carefully removed and taken to a far distant area of the airport where it was duly "disrupted". What seemed like hours later I was asked to go and meet the bomb disposal officer at his remote location. When the bag had been blown up (disrupted) it transpired the "bomb" had been made up of an alarm clock and a set of a woman's electrical hair curlers made from long sticks of foam, complete with curly wires going to a plug.

The owner eventually came back to claim her suitcase, only to be given a large black bin bag with many pieces of shattered plastic and damaged clothes. She left with a stern warning not to leave bags unattended at busy airports in future. So, when is a bomb not a bomb? Well, when it is a set of hair curlers and an alarm clock of course.

An ex-colleague, Dave Lock, had also worked at Gatwick airport police division. He reminded me of how some officers viewed "suspicious bags". Some would take a devil may care approach and just wander over to a suitcase, kick it a few times then pronounce "No, it's not a bomb" Whilst others would take a little more effort as the following story in Dave's own words will show.

As Dave says; "One morning I was on foot patrol airside, which I think was 6 beat. Off chirps the radio sending me to the outbound baggage belts, where a loader pointed out a suspicious bag to me on the now stationary system. I obviously asked why it was suspicious and he told me to listen to it. Leaning towards it, I could hear an obvious buzzing sound coming from within. There had recently been an instruction on suspicious bags, which required me to call a supervisor, which I duly did.

Instead of a Sergeant, I was blessed by the approach of an Inspector, who I will call "Bob". The Inspector told me that he didn't like the look of it and, after ascertaining that if had previously been moved by the loader, decided to pick it up himself. Everyone nearby took several steps back. He examined the bag which was securely locked, so he decided to remove the bag from the hall.

Using his quick thinking, he commandeered a nearby loader, together with luggage trucks and placed the bag on the empty truck.

He then instructed the loader to convey him and the bag to a different part of the airport which he seemed to think would be safe. In doing so they crossed several live taxiways to his place of safety, which was near the fuel farm of all places.

 Needless to say that after breaking into the bag an electric razor was found to be the culprit. The following morning at the briefing there was a "kangaroo court" and "Bob" was charged with several offences. He put in a guilty plea and we all had a laugh."

Normally "daft behaviour" such as this at a traditional police station would warrant the supply of free doughnuts to the whole team of officers at the next briefing. However, In the late 1980s each of the four "sections" at Gatwick amounted to upwards of thirty or forty staff, which could have proved rather expensive for the hapless inspector.

When introducing this section for my police talks, I would show a photograph of Richard Reid. That name probably means nothing to most people without an accompanying picture of a rather dishevelled young man with a beard, wearing a fetching orange US prison jump suit. The press nicknamed him "The Shoe Bomber".

On 22 December 2001, Reid boarded American Airlines Flight 63 at Paris on a flight to Miami. He was wearing shoes packed with about ten ounces of high explosives, which he unsuccessfully tried to detonate in flight. He was subdued by other passengers and the aircraft was re- routed to Logan International Airport in Boston, Massachusetts, the closest US airport. He was arrested, charged, and indicted. In 2002 he pleaded guilty to eight counts of terrorism. Reid was sentenced to three life terms plus 110 years in prison without parole, together with fines of $2 million.

Talks experience

I was just introducing this section of my talk at a meeting in Bromley when a lady suddenly called out from the back row "Richard, Richard" as I showed his full-face picture. I was quite startled, as nothing like this had ever happened before.

The way she had said his name it was clear to me she knew Richard Reid personally. I asked her how on earth she knew him. She told me that he had been her neighbour and had lived in the town where I was standing that day: Bromley.

The lady then said a fascinating thing. She said "What a helpful boy". She quite clearly had no idea what he had gone on to do in later life. I was very naughty and asked her if she had seen Richard lately (knowing full well that he was incarcered in a super maximum security prison in Colorado, USA).She replied "Oh no dear, has he been in trouble?" Yes, just a bit!

A few months later a similar thing happened. I was at a National Trust supporters group in Eastbourne. As soon as the slide of Richard Reid came on the screen, a lady on the third row called out "Oh that's Richard Reid".

I said, "Don't tell me, you used to live in Bromley". She replied, "No dear, I have never been to Bromley". I then asked her how on earth she had remembered the Shoe Bombers real name after all these years.

 "It's very easy for me, dear as my name is Mrs Reid and this is my husband Richard" she said, pointing to the man sitting next to her!

"The rough boys want another ladder, sir"

On 5th May 1980 members of the SAS (Special Air Service Regiment) successfully raided the Iranian embassy in Princess Gate, London after a six day stand-off with terrorists. The six terrorists had seized twenty six hostages and the world watched in anticipation as Margaret Thatcher's government grappled with a very serious situation.

Following countless rehearsals by the SAS and the murder of one of the hostages, the order was given for the embassy to be stormed. Who can forget the live TV pictures of the troopers abseiling down ropes and entering the embassy, which by that time had its curtains on fire.

One hostage sadly died as did five of the six gunmen. The final gunman was convicted at court and released from prison on parole in 2008. He now lives in south London. He had tried to smuggle himself out of the embassy pretending to be a hostage, but was spotted.

I mentioned the word _rehearsal_ for good reason, as back in late 1989 I was the Armed Unit Inspector at Gatwick airport. One day half of my unit turned up for an evening shift only to be told to go immediately to a waiting British Airways Boeing 747 Jumbo jet near the South Terminal. Together we all walked aboard to find it totally deserted, except for the full complement of crew. We were told to strap ourselves in, but not told why or where we were going.

It was dark when we landed only a short time later. Some aircraft steps were wheeled up to the door and I remember walking off the aircraft behind a senior British Airways manager. I shall never forget his conversation with a junior colleague who had run up the steps to meet him in a state of high agitation.

"Excuse me sir" the man said "The rough boys want another set of aircraft steps". The manager's response was immediate and to the point; "Give the rough boys whatever they want. I just don't want my aircraft damaged!"

It suddenly dawned on us all who we were going to be working with that night. My thoughts flooded back to that evening in May 1980. Suffice to say my team's job was to form a security cordon around the Boeing 747 we had flown up on after some three hundred or so young army cadets had been shepherded on board to simulate passengers.

Suddenly, over to our left there was a huge explosion and flash of flame set off as a distraction. At the same time out of the blackness came helicopters with dark figures abseiling down ropes onto the roof of the aircraft. A few muffled bangs came from within the aircraft.

Within minutes the doors of the aircraft were thrown open and the cadets were bundled off only to be handcuffed and segregated by my officers. This might seem harsh, but you will remember the surviving Iranian Embassy siege terrorist had pretended to be one of his victims back in 1980 and we couldn't take any chances.

At the end of this exercise we flew straight back to Gatwick. To say we were impressed by the SAS was an understatement. I eventually got to bed about 5am and remember my wife asking if it had been a quiet night. The adrenalin was still pumping, so I had to tell her all about our adventure. I remember telling her how glad I was that the SAS were on our side!

Just one final aside about the Iranian Embassy siege in 1980. My favourite story from the aftermath of that event was when Margaret and Denis Thatcher travelled to Knightsbridge Barracks to congratulate the SAS troopers who had been engaged in the highly successful raid.

Apparently, someone suggested a TV should be wheeled into the room so they could all watch the re-run of proceedings. Mrs Thatcher readily agreed. A fantastic quote from the autobiography of one of the SAS men involved recounts the event.

"As the first dramatic newsreel shots were shown we crowded around the TV set shining in the darkened corner of the room. "Sit down you at the front and let the rest of us see" ordered the gruff Scottish voice of one of the SAS troopers at the rear. The Prime Minister obediently sat down cross-legged on the floor. According to one of her aids, it was the first time he had ever seen Mrs Thatcher take an order from anyone!"

A flight to freedom

It was late June 1989 and All Nippon Airways (ANA) were having a proving flight from Japan via Moscow into Gatwick Airport as this was to be a brand-new route for the company. This was to determine any potential problems with the service before it was launched.

The Boeing 747 jumbo descended into Gatwick with just a handful of staff and crew onboard instead of the many hundreds it would normally carry. It taxied to a stop and the small number of passengers began to disembark.

Two maintenance engineers went out to the now stationary plane. Let's call them Bill and Jim. While Bill went clockwise around the giant aircraft, checking on various areas, his colleague Jim walked in the opposite direction

Time was getting on and Bill reached the wheel area under one of the wings. He looked up and saw Jim's leg sticking out of the wheel well.

"Come on down it's time for a cup of tea" he shouted up to his colleague. At which point Jim tapped him on the shoulder from behind, making poor Bill jump out of his skin. "So if that's not your leg up there, whose is it?" said Bill

That's when a call came into the Police Control room at the airport. A set of wheels was rolled over to the underside of the wing. Inside the wheel-well we discovered a young man, aged twenty one. He was a Russian national.

What I shall always remember is the sight of the man called Igor lying there completely still but looking so at peace. He had with him a pair of sun glasses, his Russian Army discharge papers showing he was a tractor driver (third class) and that he had just completed a tour of duty in Afghanistan. He also had a letter from the American Embassy in Moscow declining his request to emigrate to that country. The only other possessions I can recall were a lightweight metal knife fork and spoon set, as used by the army and a Bible.

Poor Igor wasn't visibly injured in any way, but had clearly died either from hyperthermia or as a result of a lack of oxygen. As the BBC reported at the time: "A Russian man was found dead in the undercarriage of a plane arriving from Moscow at Gatwick airport. A postmortem found that he died from a lack of oxygen at high altitude." Perhaps Igor had read reports of young people escaping in this way from Cuba to the USA. But that is a much shorter route and at a much lower altitude.

As you can imagine we were visited fairly rapidly by heavily built men from the Russian Embassy in London, eager to repatriate the body. More urgently they wanted to find out how on earth a young man could breach security at Moscow Airport, enabling him to scramble onto the wheel well of an international jet.

Tragically, a mere four months later on the 9th November 1989 the Berlin Wall was opened for East Germans to walk freely into the west. The thaw within the USSR under President Gorbachov allowed greater freedom.

However, it is unclear whether Igor Litvinenko (the stowaway) would ever have been allowed to follow his dream of a new life in the USA.

Our stowaway shared the surname with another Russian who would make headlines a few years later. Alexander Litvinenko, was a Russian defector and former officer of the Russian FSB secret service. In 2000 he fled with his family to London and was granted asylum in the United Kingdom, where he worked as a journalist, writer and consultant for the British intelligence service.

On November 1st 2006 he suddenly fell ill and was hospitalised in London. It was established as a case of poisoning by radioactive polonium-210; he died from this on 23 November..

Interestingly, some years later a similar stowaway incident occurred but this time it was at Heathrow airport. In June 2010 the BBC reported that a Romanian stowaway had been freed by police after being cautioned.

"A stowaway was arrested after landing at Heathrow Airport. The Romanian stowaway, who flew from Vienna to Heathrow Airport, whilst hiding in a private jet's wheel compartment, has been freed by police without charge". The 20-year-old man was arrested when he fell out of the rear wheel cavity as the jet landed at the west London airport on Sunday evening.

He had bruises and hypothermia from outside temperatures as low as -41C. But experts said the stowaway survived the flight because the plane flew at a low altitude to avoid stormy weather.

The aircraft belonged to a sheikh from the United Arab Emirates and had been standing empty on the tarmac at the airport in Vienna, since Thursday. It flew without passengers to Heathrow. The man apparently told British authorities that he got under a fence and climbed into the undercarriage of the first plane he saw without even knowing its destination.

A Metropolitan Police spokesman said the man was arrested for stowing away in an aircraft, contrary to the Air Navigation Order 2009, but was cautioned and freed with no further action being taken.

Just while I am talking about people surviving or falling from aircraft, there can be no one as lucky as Vesna Vulovic. Vesna was a Serbian air stewardess who survived the highest ever fall by a human being.

This happened after her plane broke up at 33,000ft (10,000m) She was working on a Yugoslav Airlines Douglas DC-9 on 26 January 1972 when a suspected bomb brought the plane down among mountains in Czechoslovakia. All the other twenty seven passengers and crew died.

According to investigators, Vulovic was trapped by a food cart in the plane's tail section as it plummeted to earth in freezing temperatures. The tail section landed in a heavily wooded and snow-blanketed part of a mountainside, which was thought to have cushioned the impact.

After arriving in hospital, Vulovic fell into a coma for 10 days. She had a fractured skull, two crushed vertebrae and she had broken her pelvis, several ribs and both legs. The fall gained her a place in the Guinness Book of Records in 1985 for the highest fall survived without a parachute. She was awarded her certificate by none other than Paul Mcartney (I suspect she might have been a secret Beatles fan)

The stewardess was temporarily paralysed from the waist down by the fall but, in time, she made a near-full recovery and returned to work for the airline in a ground based desk job.

She never regained any memory of the accident or of her rescue, she said, and continued to fly as a passenger frequently saying, "People always want to sit next to me on the plane," she said. I wonder why?

The very expensive sleepover.

In the summer of 1988 there were numerous disruptions to travel due to IRA bomb calls. For instance there was the 1997 Grand National debacle. With just two phone calls, the IRA succeeded in forcing 70,000 people to leave the racetrack at Aintree, the annual venue for the country's premier horse-racing event. The meeting was cancelled. 250 million viewers around the world had been waiting to watch the race on TV and many millions of pounds of bets had been wagered.

 After the evacuation and extensive searches, no bombs were found and the steeplechase was run two days later. The hoax calls at Aintree were the culmination of ten days of IRA actions Many other incidents of coded calls to the emergency services have led to massive disruption on roads, rail and at airports.

The problem, of course, is judging what is and what isn't a genuine call. Would you want to be the one to make that decision?

It was around 8am one summer's day in1988. As the duty Inspector for Gatwick airport police that day, I had just started my refreshment break in the airport's staff canteen. I was reflecting on how I had enjoyed my first week with my new team of around fifty officers (half of whom were armed). Working in a commercial environment was certainly new to me after ten years with Sussex police.

My radio crackled and I was asked to call the main airport telephone exchange urgently. The operator then told me they had received a call about a flight which was due to depart shortly for one of the Arab Gulf States.

The male caller had stated there was a bomb planted in the hold of the aircraft and, if they knew what was best for them, the 'plane shouldn't take off'. The operator then very calmly said the words I shall never forget, "Well Inspector....do you wish to declare an "Act of Aggression (ground)?"

After only a handful of days at the airport and with limited experience, this certainly was a critical moment and one which took my mind off my rapidly cooling bacon and eggs.

Luckily, during my induction training at Gatwick I had photocopied a number of documents and then reduced them in size to fit into one of my many jacket pockets. One such document explained the meaning of such weird terms as;

Full Emergency: when an aircraft has notified a potential problem and the police, the ambulance service and Fire brigade all take up designated positions......(just in case).

Aircrash imminent: yet another call you don't want to hear when you are on duty

Finally, on my list: *Act of Aggression (ground)*

So, what to do? As calmly as possible I asked the operator to repeat the circumstances of the call and whether in fact such a flight existed. She replied that yes, indeed a 'plane with the flight number given was due to depart in the next hour and it was destined for one of the Arab Gulf States.

"Oh yes" she said, "And by the way...the hold contains some of the King of Saudi Arabia's art collection." I took a final look at the list of criteria which determined an Act of Aggression (ground) and said as firmly as I could "Yes, I authorise that state".

There was quite a long pause at the other end of the line and then she said "Very well" and hung up, but not before taking a note of my name and warrant number. No doubt, ready for the public enquiry when it all went horribly wrong!

I honestly thought I had done my bit and went back to my cold bacon and eggs. Suddenly, the air was full of sirens and fire engines and ambulances tearing along the road outside.

It was only when a fellow Inspector called me up and asked what on earth I had done that I realised this had been quite a "bold" step to take:.....his words, not mine! The upshot of this story was even more curious.

For security reasons the aircraft was towed to the far end of the airport. Then all the baggage was offloaded onto the tarmac and checked. Thankfully, it wasn't raining with all those art treasures. The rush of fire engines and ambulances was just in case the aircraft went "Bang".

Unknown to me at the time, in those days it was common practice to dispatch a couple of plain clothes detectives to the check-in desk relating to the bomb call. On their way they had popped into the airport telephone exchange and listened intently to the actual recorded message.

They had then gone to stand near the check-in desk in the terminal for the relevant flight. A short time later (and well after the designated closing time for checking in) a young man and woman had casually approached the desk.

The man asked the check in agent if it was still possible for his girlfriend to catch her flight. The detectives instantly recognised the softly spoken Arabic voice. One officer took him aside and the other officer spoke independently to the young woman.

Very quickly it became clear that the couple had overslept that morning. The young man very gallantly said that she shouldn't worry as he would ensure her flight didn't go without her. He then proceeded to make the fateful call and then calmly drove down to Gatwick.

What do you think happened to our Arabic Romeo? Well, he received a £20,000 bill for costs at court for the flight delay and trouble he had caused. Oh yes, and 12 months imprisonment. Indeed a very expensive sleepover!

Just a couple of final stupid incidents with bomb hoaxes. Whilst one is not airline related, it is still worth mentioning.

Neil McArdel, a twenty six year old bridegroom appeared at Liverpool Crown Court in 2013. Neil had failed to fill in the correct paperwork for his planned wedding at the local Register Office. Rather than confess to his bride to be, he made a call saying, "This is not a hoax call. There's a bomb in St Georges Hall and it will go off in 45 minutes"

The hall was evacuated. Bride, Amy Williams, was left standing outside in her wedding dress with all the other wedding guests. Police traced the call and McArdel was arrested the same day, quickly admitting the offence and saying he was embarrassed and ashamed. That didn't influence the trial judge who sentenced him to 12 months imprisonment. On the positive side, Amy said she would stand by her man. I assume she will be doing all the organising for the next wedding ceremony!

Back in 2011 Kevin Flynn, 31 a chef from Worthing, made a hoax call claiming his estranged wife was about to board a 'plane with a bomb. He told police the device was being taken on a New York-bound aircraft by his wife Kerensa at either Heathrow or Gatwick.

He had made the anonymous call after the couple decided to end their relationship. He said he wanted her stopped and humiliated after he found she'd damaged some of his belongings whilst packing her suitcase for the trip to New York. He was jailed for 12 months

Gatwick's amazing coincidence.

We have all, no doubt heard the old saying "Practice makes perfect". Working at Gatwick proved the ideal place for me and my officers to practice for incidents which we hoped would never actually happen.

For instance, every year the airport has to run a re-licencing exercise to simulate various emergencies. Sometimes the most amazing coincidences occur and this is exactly what happened one winters evening in 1989. It was about 6pm and a large-scale exercise had been planned to simulate a firearms incident.

We had a number of extra officers at the police station and even some specially trained firearms support dogs.

The briefing for the exercise was scheduled for 7pm. All of a sudden, I heard a message come over the radio. I will never forget the calm voice passing the information. It was an elderly Traffic Warden who was working near the South Terminal. "Traffic Warden 1-3 to control, over". "Go ahead Traffic Warden 1-3, over" "I don't want to worry you, but a member of the public has just told me there is a person on the roof of car park 3 with a gun looking down onto the passengers. Over."

As you might expect there was a brief stunned silence in the control room and I asked them to get the Traffic warden to repeat his message. This he did, word for word the same. I couldn't believe it, as the exercise was not due to start until after 8pm.

Armed officers were sent to the area and, true enough, they too could just about make out a shape on the roof of the multi-story car park with what looked like a gun. It was definitely _not_ part of the planned exercise. Amazingly, we had all the resources we needed to hand. The area was sealed off, passengers and staff evacuated and cordons set up. Some of the armed officers got into position with a good view of the gunman. The suspect was dressed in camouflage gear with a black face mask.

After a short while it was decided that one of the Firearms Support dogs (a German Shepherd) should be sent in to tackle the suspect. This was incredibly effective and the gun was dropped without anyone getting harmed. Armed officers shouted orders to remain still and moved in to arrest the gunman.

He was handcuffed and then searched for other weapons and possible explosives. It was only as the officers were carrying out a thorough body search that they encountered something they were not expecting. It wasn't a hand grenade, a large knife or explosives. They suddenly realised the gun-MAN was in fact a WOMAN ! The gun she was waving about was actually an imitation, but oh so realistic, especially in the dark.

It transpired that this Irish lady had bought the clothes, balaclava and gun in London and travelled to Gatwick, as she knew there were permanently

155

armed police officers on duty twenty four hours a day. Little did she know she had picked entirely the wrong day to visit Gatwick, but it made for a very realistic "exercise". It was strongly suspected she'd intended to commit what has become known as "Suicide by Cop". This is quite widespread in the USA but far less so in the UK, thank goodness.

It is defined as is a suicide method in which a suicidal individual deliberately behaves in a threatening manner, with intent to provoke a lethal response from a law enforcement officer.

I mentioned earlier that "D" section at Gatwick had a selection of characters and that keeping moral high was important, as boredom could soon creep in. I was forever encouraging my Sergeants to monitor and motivate where possible. Occasionally funny things happened including the following incident.

I was on a night shift when, around midnight, I decided it was time I met up (or made an RV...rendezvous) with one of my young officers. I called up the control room to get them to find his location.

Let's just call him Pc JT to save his embarrassment. The young officer said he was patrolling the Cargo village, so I suggested I would join him outside the main hanger in about thirty minutes.

I drove around to the Cargo area and located where I thought we had agreed to meet. There was no sign of Pc JT. I got out of the car and started to wander around the well lit area which I had always found fascinating, even when I was a Pc myself assigned to this area back in 1981. Another ten minutes went by, but still no officer.

I asked the control room to give me the "talk through" facility so I could speak direct to the officer, as I was beginning to get a little worried about him. I called him up to check his location. All I heard was a very echoey voice telling me that he was locked in the gents toilet in the cargo handlers office block.

Ten minutes later I managed to locate him and found that he was indeed stuck and could not get the cubicle door to open from the inside. It transpired that as he had entered the cubicle, he had been rather too vigorous with the handle, slammed it and the whole mechanism and spindle had become detached, falling off on the _outside_ of the toilet.

Luckily, I managed to find all the relevant pieces, reassembled it and released the unfortunate officer. I thought it would be funny to compose a message for the station briefing file warning (in a lighthearted manner) about the dangers of this type of incident. I was intending to read this out just to my D section officers the following night, as a joke.

The message read: _From Superintendent "G" Division   To; All supervisors_

Following a rather embarrassing incident in the gentlemen's toilet at Timberham House in the Cargo area involving a Gatwick officer, it has been decided that in future all "D" section officers will only make visits to public toilets in pairs. A collection of spare keys, door handles and spindles will be kept in the Landside patrol car for immediate use on receipt of a coded message "W.C 10/26" from any officer in distress.

I typed this up, printed off a copy and went home to bed. When I got to work that evening, I was summoned to the Superintendent's office to explain why he appeared to have authorised some crazy new order regarding toilet visits. Unfortunately for me, the message I had jokingly created had in fact gone to all the other printers and been placed on other briefing files for all and sundry to read: whoops!

As a footnote, PcJT didn't let the toilet incident stand in his way. He emigrated and rose rapidly through the ranks in the Western Australia police force, finally becoming a Commander responsible for Counter Terrorism and Emergency Response.

One of the officers on D section was an excellent artist and she produced the below cartoon entitled "An affectionate look at D section".

Look carefully at top right and you may see *"David Bellamy, alias Neil Sadler deep in the jungle of paperwork!"*. (Amanda Smith 1989)

As a final paragraph to working at Gatwick, all agencies needed to work together in order for the airport to function efficiently. Many joint exercises were held and liaison meetings kept relationships running smoothly (for the most part). That didn't stop the odd "high jinks" between colleagues, as the following story shows. I have agreed with the "informant" not to reveal either his name or the section of Sussex Police to which he was attached at the time.

"On one occasion, I got some of those kids sweets that dyed your mouth purple. Early one morning, shortly before the Lagos flight arrival, I discreetly put one on every immigration officers (IO) desk in the arrivals hall. The arrivals hall filled up and every immigration desk was manned. I watched as virtually every IO picked up the candy and started to suck it. Very soon every IO had purple lips and tongues. Of course, they knew nothing, but probably wondered why the in bound passengers from Nigeria had such puzzled expressions on their faces.

When things quietened down I followed one IO back to his office and watched as he opened his lunch box and began to eat a sandwich. He took a bite, looked at the sandwich and saw that, around the tooth marks, the bread was stained purple.

He panicked, dropped the sandwich and ran off to the restrooms. Soooo funny. For a few days I expected consequences, but those who knew kept the secret and it all blew over."

Chapter 13

"Were you ever scared or injured?"

These were questions I have been asked frequently during or after police talks. Well, the answer is yes to both questions.

Thirty years would have been an extremely long time to go without some form of disquiet at work, not to say extreme panic. The funny thing I noticed about myself over the years was that I could cope quite well in times of crisis, but could frequently deal less well with mundane incidents. This was the case in both my professional as well as my private life.

When something of great importance or extreme danger arose, I seemed to be able to slow down my thinking, prioritise my actions and stay calm. That's not to say that beneath the surface my legs weren't paddling frantically, like the proverbial duck on the pond.

My very first recollection of fear was way back in 1979. I was on foot patrol in the early hours of the morning when I heard a burglar alarm start to ring. As I turned a corner, I saw the alarm was attached to the local Post Office in Bognor Regis. The front of the premises appeared to be secure, so I walked around to the rear of the parade of shops and climbed up the fire escape stairs onto the roof.

As I looked at the various sky lights, I noticed one had been smashed. It led down into the bakers shop directly next to the post office. I assumed the burglar had used this as his entrance point and then somehow managed to gain access to the post office, hence activating the alarm.

By this time some colleagues had arrived and were monitoring the front of the shops in case the burglar made a run for it. For some unknown reason, I decided to climb through the open skylight and drop down into the bakers in an attempt to arrest whoever had broken in. It was quite a tight squeeze and to do so I had to remove my rather cumbersome truncheon which I placed on the roof behind me.

As I dropped down and landed on the baker's preparation table, a cloud of flour puffed up making me cough. I then became acutely aware of a very strange smell. I honestly believed the burglar was crouching somewhere in the dimly lit workshop, as I kept catching sickly wafts of Brut aftershave; never my favourite fragrance.

This was mixed with another, even less pleasant, odour. I can still remember the hairs on the back of my neck springing upwards and thinking why on earth I had been daft enough not to bring my truncheon. I looked around and noticed a sturdy wooden rolling pin which would have to substitute.

As I crept carefully towards the rear of the bakers, I became aware of the source of the other rather nasty smell. There, by the open rear door, was a large pile of human poo, which more experienced officers later explained would have been deposited by the burglar in his heightened emotional state. Suffice to say we didn't locate the offender who had also forced the rear door of the post office. He had no doubt dropped down into the bakers by mistake.

In the late 1980s I was a uniform Inspector based at Burgess Hill police station in West Sussex. This was not quite Fort Apache, the Bronx or even Crawley or Brighton, which had far higher crime and disorder rates. However, like most towns, it did have its fair share of trouble makers.

One night I was standing in the front office checking that all calls from the public had been dealt with satisfactorily before booking off duty and driving home.

All of a sudden we heard a great deal of shouting from right outside the front entrance to the police station. Then, there was a most almighty crash as a brick was launched through the main window, followed by manic laughter and the sound of running feet.

Myself and a couple of officers ran outside and could see a man staggering up the road away from us, weaving all over the footpath and laughing to himself. One of the officers immediately identified the man as a local drunken offender with a long history of violence against the police.

As we approached the man (let's call him John, as that was his name!) he turned and started brandishing a broken cider bottle towards us.

He began shouting obscenities in a slurred Irish accent and daring us to get closer as he was looking forward to "cutting us up".

Even though there were three of us, we only had our rather pathetic fourteen inches of wooden truncheon to defend ourselves. This was long before the advent of Captor pepper spray, Taser electric stun guns or even expandable steel batons or stab proof vests.

I noticed that "John" was now standing outside the local newsagents shop. Leaning against the wall was one of those large, metal bill boards which often advertised the lead story in that day's newspaper. As he stepped away from the bill board, I walked forward quickly, picked it up and, using it as a shield, approached "John", suggesting he might like to drop the jagged bottle.

At that point he lurched towards me and I just managed to strike him with the steel bill board, resulting in him dropping the bottle and my colleagues jumping at him and handcuffing him securely.

Like many incidents, it is only afterwards that you consider what might have happened. The Inspector and the bill board incident remained part of the Burgess Hill nick folk lore for quite some time I am told.

Finally, I will link the words scared and injured together. It is an example of what can happen when a police officer is off duty but feels he needs to step into a situation. It was a chilly December day and I was in Seaford arranging the programme for a visit by an Assistant Chief Constable a few weeks later.

Wearing plain clothes, I wandered off into the town centre at lunch time to buy some last-minute items for Christmas. The town was quite busy, mostly with elderly residents out shopping. I became aware of a commotion taking place about fifty feet away from me and outside a row of shops. I could hear men's raised voices and quite a few expletives peppered the air.

I then saw two men, one younger than the other, pushing each other about, but, in the process, colliding with elderly shoppers who were looking quite distressed. I approached the two men, took out my police warrant card and told them to pack it in and if they wanted to argue, to go somewhere quieter and less public. To my surprise, they stopped the pushing and seemed to calm down.

I was then aware the older man, who must have been in his late 20s, had really bad scarring to his face. He reminded me of the horror film character Freddy Krueger, the scary fictional character in the Nightmare on Elm Street film series.

This man began to walk back up the High street, giving me the chance to ask the younger man what had been going on.

He explained that the other man had just discovered he was a police informer. He realised I was not from Seaford or I would have recognised the other chap who was a well-known trouble maker.

Suddenly, I heard the sound of a revving engine coming down the street and a white van screeched to a halt nearby. Out of the van jumped "Freddy Krueger" brandishing a pick axe handle. He looked really angry as he ran straight for me. I told the younger man to run off and dial 999 as I was going to need urgent assistance.

With that, Freddy launched himself at me. I grappled with him and we both fell across the bonnet of a stationary taxi. Time seemed to stand still, but I was aware of the sound of an approaching police car, its siren wailing. We continued to struggle on the ground but at least I had managed to loosen his grip on the pick axe handle and kicked it away into the road. A young police officer ran towards us and draw his side handled baton. I called for him to drag Freddy off me but he decided to tap him with his baton instead. I recall shouting, "Either pull him off me or f**** hit him as if you mean it"

To cut a long (and painful) story short, the older man was arrested, handcuffed and taken away. It was only as I stood up that I became aware of a really sharp pain in my right leg. In the melee, I had managed to tear my right calf muscle. This took many visits to the physiotherapist to put right and my days of playing squash were somewhat curtailed

Whilst writing this chapter the trial of three young men accused of killing Thames Valley police officer PC Andrew Harper concluded at the Old Bailey. PC Harper was dragged for more than a mile along country lanes in Berkshire after he and a colleague responded to reports of a quad bike theft on 15 August 2019, jurors heard. Their shift had officially ended four hours before.

PC Harper suffered catastrophic fatal injuries when his ankles got caught in a strap trailing behind a vehicle driven by Henry Long, 19, who admitted manslaughter but was cleared by the jury of murder. Albert Bowers and Jessie Cole, both 18, were cleared of murder but found guilty of manslaughter.

The court heard the Seat travelled for more than a mile towards the A4 before PC Harper became detached and died in the road. The defendants had been prepared to use force "if met with resistance" and the trio had in their possession a large axe, three crowbars and a hammer and were "plainly determined to steal the quad bike" from a home near Stanford Dingley.

During the trial, the prosecution said it had sought murder charges after alleging the defendants were aware the officer was being dragged behind the car. Defence lawyers claimed the incident was a "freak event" that no-one could have planned or foreseen.

PC Harper, from Wallingford, Oxfordshire, had been married to his childhood sweetheart for just four weeks before his death. Within weeks, he and his wife had been due to have their honeymoon in the Maldives.

Speaking after the verdicts, Mrs Lissie Harper said: "No sentence or verdict will ever bring my incredible, selfless and heroic husband back. The results from this trial I had hoped would bring justice - but in reality make no difference to the heart-wrenching pain I will continue to feel for the rest of my life."

Reading the summary of this tragic case affected me greatly. I thought back to January 13th 1979 when Julie and I had been married in the snow at Stoke Prior, Worcestershire. Had what happened to Andrew Harper happened to me (which it quite easily could have done on a few occasions) Julie would have been a widow by St Valentine's day 1979.

This and far too many other tragic cases of police officers killed on duty emerge into the public consciousness and then subside when new stories appear. However, there is one organisation which will never let such tragedies be forgotten. The Police Memorial Trust was formed on the 3rd May, 1984 by Film Producer Michael Winner. Its formation was almost accidental. Deeply moved by the death of Metropolitan police officer Yvonne Fletcher in St. James's Square, Winner wrote a letter to The Times that was published on 21 April, 1984, suggesting that a memorial be erected.

"It would serve to indicate that not everyone in this country takes seeming pleasure in attacking the Police in the execution of their difficult duties, but that most of us regard their conduct and bravery, under a whole series of endless and varied provocations, as demonstrably noble and worthy of our thanks", he wrote.

When the letter was printed Mr Winner received donations from the public together with a large number of letters approving of his sentiments. A few days later, on the 27th April, at the invitation of Sir David English, the Editor of the Daily Mail, Winner wrote a long article in that newspaper on the day of Yvonne's funeral. The article finished with the words: –

"I can see a day in the future when human memory, being what it is, has discarded the events that now seem so important, and the shadows from the trees above sway slowly to and fro on the pavement of St James's Square, the sunlight catching a small Memorial.

"Maybe two people passing by will stop and one will say to the other – "Yvonne Fletcher? Who was she?" "To which there is a simple and noble answer: She was a member of the British Police Force."

So the Police Memorial Trust was formed. Its aims were to erect memorials to police officers killed in the course of their hazardous duty, usually on the spot where they met their death. This new idea attracted considerable attention with donations pouring in from ordinary people, from members of the Cabinet, MPs. members of the House of Lords, film stars, institutions and many of the biggest businesses in the land.

The Trust had its first memorial to Yvonne Fletcher unveiled in St. James's Square on 1st February 1985. In a rare display of political solidarity the leaders of all the main political parties attended the unveiling, which was performed by the Prime Minister, Mrs Margaret Thatcher. Since the formation of the Trust in 1984 it has erected 49 local memorials to 48 Police Officers killed in their execution of their hazardous duty, normally at or near where they fell.

In addition, the National Police Memorial can be found at the junction of the Mall and Horse guards in Westminster, London. This was designed by Lord Foster of Thames Bank and opened by HM The Queen in April 2005.It was the first memorial to be placed in St James's Park for over one hundred years and against strong opposition. Michael Winner fought for over ten years to obtain planning permission and then funded the memorial's construction personally at a cost of over one million pounds.

There are currently fifty names recorded on it from all over the UK. The oldest commemorates a Constable James Armstrong who died on 30th September 1847 aged 40 years in the Lake district. His endorsement reads:

"Constable Armstrong was killed while carrying out his hazardous duties. On his way home he stopped for refreshments at The Royal Hotel, Dockray to obtain directions and to continue his arduous journey on foot, to the obtaining and executing of a warrant.

He later became lost in the dark and instead of keeping to the road during his disorientated route his path took him high up to Wanthwaite Crag. Whilst attempting to retrace his steps he fell resulting in his tragic death".

As a retired Sussex officer, I was interested in the only mention of my old force. PC Jeffrey Tooley, aged 26 was killed on 24th April 1999. His citation reads;

"PC Tooley was mown down by a van when carrying out speed enforcement in an attempt to reduce road casualties.". His memorial stands at the side of the main A259 road in Shoreham, West Sussex.

As someone once said to me once, "It's not like working in Tescos; you never know what is coming next". Sadly, for some former colleagues, they leave home for work one day and never return.

Finally, on a more upbeat note to conclude this chapter, I mentioned retirement above.

After thirty years service I decided to retire in September 2008. At the time I was seconded to the National Police Training organisation as a Regional Implementation officer for a training programme. All my work colleagues gathered to say farewell and Trefor, whom I had worked closely with, made an excellent speech. He handed me a CD of songs compiled by my workmates and which they associated with me. These included; The title music to the Magnificent Seven to remind me of all the Best Western hotels he and I had stayed in whilst travelling the country. Also, "Rosie and Jim" title music as the team knew I was hoping to buy a share in a canal narrow boat, etc

CLDP
Hits to
remember
us by

Trefor handed me a yellow jacket worn by police officers at the scene of road crashes. The badge on the back had been "doctored" to read Paddling Pool Inspector. Trefor then took great delight in regaling everyone with the story behind this "gift".

In May that year he and I had agreed to attend the Police Federation conference at Bournemouth. We had booked rooms at a local hotel which had a leisure complex complete with swimming pool. I arrived at the hotel first and decided to make the most of the facilities before the hard work started later that evening. I went to the spa check in area and was given my towel and directed to the changing rooms. I then had a fantastic swim as I had the whole pool to myself. I spotted a jacuzzi and climbed in. As I lay in the shallow, warm water I couldn't figure out how to start the bubbles. I kept pressing what I thought were buttons but nothing seemed to work.

It was then time to get changed and as I walked out of the reception area the two young men were staring at me in a strange way. I thought I had better tell them their jacuzzi was out of order, only for both men to start sniggering and tell me they didn't actually have a jacuzzi. They had been observing me for ten minutes on their CCTV system whilst I lay in the children's paddling pool! Cue a rapid exit and a yellow jacket with a doctored title on the back for retirement!

Chapter 14

And finally

So, the government imposed "lock down" was easing. Life was very slowly getting back to some form of normality. If I hear the phrase "We must get used to the new normal" once more I will scream!

As I write this in late-summer 2020, my live talks have still not resumed due to problems with "social distancing" (yet another new phrase in our ever expanding twenty first century lexicon). When I checked my records, I had completed some 840 talks since 2012. Only a few months before the arrival of the Covid-19 pandemic my wife had asked me what on earth I would do when the bookings dried up. Sadly, I was now about to find out.

Fortunately, a new tech-based start-up company called Mirthy got in touch and asked me if I would consider creating on-line pre-recorded talks. I was a bit slow off the mark initially but then, having watched another speaker "perform" from his living room, I really embraced it. So much so that I recorded five different talks with one in costume (a pretend convicts set, normally used for Stag weekends I suspect)

Mirthy's website stated: Mirthy is an online platform for professional public speakers, often retirees themselves, to provide online talks to older adults in the comfort of their homes.

Their aim was to reduce social isolation amongst older people. They had secured a contract with McCarthy and Stone, retirement flat developers, to provide entertaining talks straight to residents' laptops or tablets. I was also encouraged to contact some of the organisations who had cancelled bookings due to the on-going health situation, in case they might be interested in this new method of delivery.

It was a totally new experience, looking into the camera of my laptop computer and talking to myself. No audience to bounce off, no elderly people to nod off, no mobile phones to ring at an inopportune moment, no one dashing off early to catch the last bus to Little Dribbling. But, on the up-side, there was no travelling for an hour and a half on the blooming M25 at rush hour.

My first talk was via the Youtube application to one hundred and seventy signed up attendees from McCarthy and Stone developments all across the UK. On the area of the website which allowed on-line chat I saw people typing greetings and messages from as far north as Glasgow (where Anthea told us the weather was sunny but windy!) down to Maldon, Virginia Water and Exeter. After my pre-recorded talk "A policeman's lot can be quite an interesting one" it was my turn to answer any questions the attendees may had typed.

These included

"Were you ever frightened?"

"What rank did you achieve?"

"Did your "underlings" really call you Guv, just like in the Sweeny?"

"What were the worst incidents to attend?"

However, my all-time favourite comment on the chat room thread that day was:

 "Sorry, just got to pop outside to mow the lawn as the bin men are coming tomorrow!" Why not keep that little nugget to yourself and just do it?

One of the aspects of the "lock down" associated with the Covid -19 pandemic was that the relationship between police officers and the public was always going to be an invidious one

On the one hand, the Government hurriedly passed new laws banning "unnecessary" journeys and only allowing the public to leave their homes for one period of exercise a day. To prevent hoards of people rushing to the likes of Hastings and Brighton on one of the many warm bank holidays, police set up road checks and turned around many drivers.

The roads became much less busy for a few weeks. So much so that the Kent, Surrey and Sussex Air Ambulance Trust reported the number of road crashes it had attended in one particular week had plummeted from 49% of its call outs to just 14%. Sadly, some people thought this gave then the green light to increase their speeds on the now much emptier public roads. In fact, according to the BBC website, over the May bank holiday weekend in 2020 Sussex police caught over six hundred motorist who were speeding. The record is currently held by a driver on the M23 near Crawley who filmed himself travelling in his Audi at 202 mph.

The internet and Facebook in particular, tried to keep everyone amused during the pandemic and a number of police speed related jokes appeared. My favourite showed a young, flash driver who had been pulled over by a Traffic officer in an aging police Volvo estate.

The man had been ostensibly driving a Bugatti Veyron, some models of which can reach top speeds of a ridiculous 253 mph.

Police officer: "Do you know why I've stopped you today sir?"

Bugatti driver; "Because I let you, officer"